OF SPEECH
NT FREEDOM FRO
OM OF WORSHIP
DOM FROM FEA
OF WORSHIP FRE
WANT FREEDO
EEDOM FROM W
DOM FROM FEAR
WORSHIP FREE

Franklin Delano Roosevelt

Books by Alan Brinkley

Voices of Protest: Huey Long, Father Coughlin, and the Great Depression

The End of Reform: New Deal Liberalism in Recession and War

Liberalism and Its Discontents

The Unfinished Nation: A Concise History of the American People

American History: A Survey

Franklin Delano Roosevelt

⁊

Alan Brinkley

Published in Association with the American Council of Learned Societies

OXFORD
UNIVERSITY PRESS
2010

OXFORD
UNIVERSITY PRESS

Oxford University Press, Inc., publishes works that further
Oxford University's objective of excellence
in research, scholarship, and education.

Oxford   New York
Auckland Cape Town Dar es Salaam Hong Kong Karachi
Kuala Lumpur Madrid Melbourne Mexico City Nairobi
New Delhi Shanghai Taipei Toronto

With offices in
Argentina Austria Brazil Chile Czech Republic France Greece
Guatemala Hungary Italy Japan Poland Portugal Singapore
South Korea Switzerland Thailand Turkey Ukraine Vietnam

Copyright © 2010 by Oxford University Press and
the American Council of Learned Societies

Published by Oxford University Press, Inc.
198 Madison Avenue, New York, NY 10016

www.oup.com

The Library of Congress Cataloging-in-Publication Data
Brinkley, Alan.
Franklin Delano Roosevelt / Alan Brinkley.
p. cm.
Published in association with the American Council of Learned Societies.
Includes bibliographical references.
ISBN 978-0-19-973202-9 (acid-free paper)
1. Roosevelt, Franklin D. (Franklin Delano), 1882–1945.
2. Presidents—United States—Biography.
I. American Council of Learned Societies.   II. Title.
E807.B75 2010   973.917092—dc22
[B]   2009027690

3 5 7 9 8 6 4 2
Printed in the United States of America
on acid-free paper

To the memories of
Frank Freidel
Arthur M. Schlesinger Jr.
David Herbert Donald
Mentors, Colleagues, Friends

Contents

Preface

Franklin Delano Roosevelt may be the most chronicled man of the twentieth century. He led the United States through the worst economic crisis in the life of the nation and through the greatest and most terrible war in human history. His extraordinary legacy, compiled during dark and dangerous years, remains alive in our own, troubled new century as an inspiring and creative model to many, and as a symbol of excessive government power to many others.

My own awareness of Roosevelt began when I was a child growing up in Washington, D.C., in the 1950s, where the image of FDR was still very much alive. My father, a journalist, had attended some of Roosevelt's Oval Office press conferences during World War II, and for the rest of his life he remembered them as among the most memorable events of his very eventful life. My mother, a Washington native, never met Roosevelt, but she nevertheless considered him an important figure in her life. I remember her devouring the three volumes of Arthur Schlesinger's *The Age of Roosevelt*—which I avidly read as well, years later. Whenever we drove down Pennsylvania Avenue, she would point out the plain granite block in front of the National Archives with the words "Franklin Delano Roosevelt"—and nothing else—inscribed on it. He had requested that it be his only monument in Washington. (Beginning in 1997, it was overshadowed by the elaborate Roosevelt Memorial near the National Mall.)

When I was in college, working on a senior thesis, I made my first trip to the Roosevelt Library in Hyde Park, New York—the nation's oldest presidential library, built during Roosevelt's lifetime. I was struck by its modesty. It was nothing like the grandiose marble and glass structures of many subsequent presidential sites, but a simple fieldstone structure sprawling across the pasture in front of the house in which Roosevelt had grown up. The house was, and still is, open to the public, and it suggests some of the contradictions in Roosevelt's life. It was clearly the home of a wealthy and aristocratic family, and thus very different from the homes of the millions of common people who idolized him. It was furnished by his mother in expensive, Parisian style, but on its walls were dozens of framed political cartoons and pictures of political events. And to his mother's dismay, there were often large gatherings of rumpled politicians, smoking, drinking, and talking loudly. Throughout the rooms and the grounds, there were also ramps, constructed to allow Roosevelt to move around his property in a wheelchair because his lifeless legs—unbeknownst to most of his contemporaries—could no longer carry him. A person of wealth and privilege in his youth, he grew up to be a disabled man who made his way to greatness through will power, empathy, and commitment.

During the years in which I have been a historian, I have written about many people, including some of Roosevelt's most implacable opponents. But I have found myself drawn again and again to the story of this enigmatic man, who has defied the efforts of so many people who have hoped to understand him fully. The titles of some of the books written about Roosevelt give an indication of his elusiveness and opaqueness: *The Juggler, The Lion and the Fox,* and *In Search of Roosevelt,* to name a few. In 1940 some Democrats constructed a seven-foot-high papier-mâché model of a sphinx, with the smiling face of Roosevelt, a cigarette holder set jauntily between his teeth, on its head. It was designed to represent the president's unwillingness to reveal whether he would run for an unprecedented third term as president, but it was also an apt symbol of Roosevelt's cryptic personality throughout his life.

Yet if Roosevelt's own thoughts and intentions remain obscure, his achievements are visible for all to see. No president since the nation's founding has done more to shape the character of American government, and no president since Lincoln has served through darker or more difficult times. Roosevelt thrived in crisis. It brought out both his greatness and his guile; it triggered his almost uncanny ability to communicate effectively with people of all kinds; and, at times, it helped him excoriate his enemies, and to revel in doing so.

There is no lack of biographies of Roosevelt. At least four have been published in the last five years alone. This short biography is deeply indebted to the extraordinary scholarship of the last half century and more, and I have benefited from the work of many historians as well as from my own. It will, I hope, help some readers introduce themselves to the age of the Great Depression and the New Deal, and will help others be reminded of its lasting impact on our own era.

Alan Brinkley, New York, June 2009

In 1945, shortly after Franklin Delano Roosevelt died, Woody Guthrie, the folk musician, wrote a song he titled "Dear Mrs. Roosevelt"—a song intended as both a condolence and a tribute. In it, Guthrie described some of the important events of Roosevelt's life (not all of them accurately). In one stanza, he wrote "he taught my soul to walk."

Through much of his own life, Franklin Roosevelt could not walk. But to most Americans of his generation, Guthrie among them, he seemed for a time to bestride the earth. So powerful was his impact on the world he led through the twentieth century's darkest years that the literal truth of his life often seemed less important than the powerful image he created—half purposefully, half unintentionally—in the popular imagination. Even decades later, public figures across the ideological spectrum try to seize a piece of his legacy—even at times to justify their efforts to dismantle it—without much concern about who Roosevelt actually was or what he actually did. He has become a figure of myth: a man for all seasons, all parties, and all ideologies.

But Roosevelt the man was not an icon. He was a complicated, elusive, and at times even devious figure. He was both a friend of the common people and a creature of the American aristocracy, both a great statesman and a consummate defender of his own political self-interest. He could be generous and he could be vindictive. He exhibited broad vision and petty deceit. He had millions of admirers and almost no intimates. Even those who felt closest to him knew only a small part of his carefully concealed inner self. How the United States dealt with both an economic and a global crisis reflected to a large degree Roosevelt's own curious personality and the strangely rarefied world that shaped it.

Roosevelt was born on January 30, 1882, on his family's estate in Dutchess County, New York. His father, James Roosevelt, came from (and largely modeled himself after) a long line of wealthy, landed gentlemen who dabbled in business but usually devoted no great effort to it. James himself worked at times as a railroad executive, invested in coal mines, and once took part in an unsuccessful effort to build a canal across Nicaragua. But by the time his son Franklin was born, James was fifty-three years old and relatively inactive professionally. A widower with a grown son, he was two years into a second marriage to a woman half his age. Sara Delano, Franklin's mother, was a wealthy, attractive woman acutely aware of her own and her husband's distinguished lineages. As a couple, they lived their lives and raised their child in a manner reminiscent of the English aristocracy—an effect symbolized by the elaborate remodeling of the house on their Hyde Park estate. Once a rambling and relatively modest Victorian home named "Springwood," it gradually became an imposing, formal country manor with a neoclassical stone facade.[1]

Franklin grew up in a remarkably cosseted environment, insulated from the normal experiences of most American boys, both by his family's wealth and by their intense and at times almost suffocating love. Until he was fourteen years old, he lived in a world dominated by adults: his Swiss tutors, who supervised his lessons at home or during the family's annual travels through Europe; his father, who sought to train his son in the life of a landowner and gentleman; and above all his mother, who devoted virtually all her energies to raising her only child, bathing and dressing him herself until he was eight years old and giving him only slightly more independence after that. It was a world of extraordinary comfort, security, and serenity, but also one of reticence and reserve, particularly after 1891, when James Roosevelt suffered the first of a series of heart attacks that left him a semi-invalid. Franklin responded protectively. He tried to spare his father anxiety by masking his own emotions and projecting a calm, cheerful demeanor. He would continue hiding his feelings behind a bright, charming surface for the rest of his life.[2]

In the fall of 1896, Franklin left his parents for the first time to attend Groton, a rigorous boarding school in a small Massachusetts town. The school's mission, according to its imperious headmaster, Endicott Peabody, was the training of the American elite. Groton was something of a shock to Roosevelt. He had never before attended school with other boys, nor had he ever had any close friends of his own age—and he had difficulty making them now. Physically slight, he attained little distinction in athletics, which dominated the life of the school. He did reasonably well academically, but he went through his four years at Groton as something of a lonely outsider. He was denied the principal honors of the school and was disliked by many of his classmates for what seemed to them a cocky demeanor and an irritating gregariousness.[3]

Entering Harvard College in 1900, he set out to make up for what he considered his social failures at Groton. He worked hard at making friends, ran for class office, and became president of the student newspaper, the *Harvard Crimson*, a post that was more a social distinction at the time than a journalistic one. (His own contributions to the newspaper consisted largely of banal editorials calling for greater school spirit.) And although he and his immediate family were Democrats, he became conspicuous in his enthusiasm for his distant cousin, Theodore Roosevelt, even affecting some of the president's famous mannerisms, including the wearing of a pince-nez and the frequent, hearty use of such well-known Roosevelt exclamations as "Delighted" and "Bully." But he failed to achieve what he craved above all: election to the most exclusive of the Harvard "final clubs," the Porcellian—the club to which his own father and his celebrated cousin had belonged. He joined another, less prestigious, club instead. It was, he once said, "the greatest disappointment of my life," and it continued to gnaw at him several years later. In 1906, when he attended his cousin Alice Roosevelt's wedding at the White House, he watched the president jovially summon his fellow Porcellians (among them Alice's new husband, Nicholas Longworth) to a closed-door meeting from which Franklin was painfully excluded.[4]

During Roosevelt's first year at Harvard, his ailing father died, and Sara Roosevelt took a house in Boston to be near her son. Franklin was devoted to his mother and always attentive and loving toward her. But he was beginning to rebel against her efforts to control him— efforts that were buttressed by her iron grip on the family finances and her unwillingness (up to her death in 1941) to allow her son any real financial independence. (Even as president, Franklin continued to receive an "allowance" from his mother.) His years at Harvard were the beginning of his lifelong effort to balance her expectations against his own determination to create a life of his own. Unwilling to challenge her openly, he did so covertly, intensifying his already well-developed secretiveness. Indeed, he obscured from his mother the most important experience of his Harvard years, his courtship of a distant cousin, Eleanor Roosevelt, the president's niece.[5]

Franklin and Eleanor had known each other slightly as children, and they began to spend time together during the 1902 social season in New York, when Eleanor made her debut. Few suspected at the time that he was becoming attracted to her. The handsome, charming, and somewhat glib Franklin seemed to have little in common with Eleanor, a quiet, reserved, and intensely serious young woman who struggled all her life to mask the insecurities she had acquired in a lonely childhood during which both her parents had died. But Franklin likely saw in her the qualities of commitment, compassion, and intellect that he feared he himself lacked. The mutual attraction grew. By the time Franklin graduated from Harvard in 1904, they were secretly engaged. When he finally told Sara of his plans, she tried to dissuade him, convinced that Eleanor lacked the poise and self-assurance that she believed were appropriate for her son. But Franklin stood firm. He and Eleanor were married in New York on March 17, 1905, in a ceremony at which Theodore Roosevelt, who gave his niece away, was the real center of attention. Over the next decade, Franklin and Eleanor had a daughter and five sons, one of whom died in infancy.[6]

By the time of his marriage, Roosevelt was a student at Columbia Law School. He did not complete the requirements for a degree, but he passed his bar exams and spent several years desultorily practicing law in New York City. He was already principally interested in politics, and in 1910 he accepted an invitation from Democratic Party leaders in Dutchess County to run for the state senate—an invitation based, like many other political opportunities he would encounter in his early career, on his position both as a county aristocrat and as a man whose name (and marriage) linked him to the most magnetic political figure of the age. The race seemed hopeless at first, for Dutchess County was staunchly Republican. But Roosevelt profited from a split in the Republican Party and from his own energetic denunciation of party bosses. He narrowly won the election.

Roosevelt made few friends at first among his fellow legislators, most of whom considered him naïve and arrogant. Surrounded by tough, pragmatic politicians who had fought their way up from obscurity, Roosevelt, with his self-consciously upper-class accent and diction, his expensive clothes, and his disconcerting tendency to speak with his chin jutting out and his nose in the air, stood out as a fey aristocrat. Many of his colleagues considered him a lightweight, even a fraud; some took to calling him (playing on his initials) "Feather Duster" Roosevelt. But he compiled a creditable, if modest, record protecting the interests of upstate farmers (his own constituents among them) and opposing Tammany Hall, the New York City Democratic machine.

In 1912 Roosevelt won reelection easily—in part because he had by then enlisted the aid of a politically knowledgeable journalist, Louis M. Howe. Howe seemed to be Roosevelt's opposite in almost every way. He was short, disheveled, withered, and in many ways coarse. He was bluntly outspoken and self-consciously gruff. But he was also a brilliant political strategist who was indispensable to Roosevelt's career for the next twenty years. Sara Roosevelt loathed him, and even Eleanor (who later came to depend on him almost as much as her husband did) felt uneasy around Howe at first. But Franklin seemed to understand instinctively that Howe could help him overcome the political limitations of his background, and he paid no attention to the complaints of his family. Howe managed Roosevelt's 1912 campaign, encouraged him to drop many of his aristocratic mannerisms, and helped him make alliances with politicians of backgrounds very different from his own. He taught Roosevelt that in politics an upper-class lineage was something to overcome, not to flaunt. He also helped fan what was already Roosevelt's strong inclination: to envision an important national political career, and even to dream of the presidency.[7]

Roosevelt did not serve out his second term in the legislature. Early in 1913, Woodrow Wilson, the new Democratic president whom Roosevelt had energetically supported, offered him an appointment as assistant secretary of the navy. Roosevelt eagerly accepted, not least because it was from that same position that Theodore Roosevelt had launched his national political career fifteen years earlier. Franklin enjoyed the new job and the Washington social life that came with it, and he plunged into both with a sometimes reckless enthusiasm. In the Navy Department, he was brashly assertive and at times almost openly insubordinate to his remarkably tolerant superior, Secretary of the Navy Josephus Daniels. Nonetheless, with the help of Howe, Roosevelt ran the day-to-day affairs of the fast-growing department with reasonable efficiency. He also kept his hand in New York politics, and in 1914 he tried (unsuccessfully) to seize the Democratic nomination for the U.S. Senate away from the Tammany candidate. From that experience he concluded that, while hostility to Tammany was good politics in Dutchess County, it was a serious, perhaps insurmountable, obstacle to statewide and national success. From 1914 on he worked to develop cordial, even if always slightly distant, relations with Tammany leaders.

Roosevelt remained in the Navy Department throughout the Wilson administration. He lobbied strenuously for preparedness during the years preceding World War I. Once the United States entered the war, he successfully promoted the laying of a large barrage of antisubmarine mines in the North Sea, supervised the production of small vessels to defend the American coasts, and intruded himself into deliberations of naval strategy and tactics that were not normally the province of the assistant secretary. He also became involved, perhaps inadvertently, in a controversy that would haunt him for years. In 1918 the navy began an attempt to "clean up" the area around the large naval base at Newport, Rhode Island, after receiving complaints about prostitution and homosexuality there. Enlisted men were dispatched to entrap sailors and others (including a prominent Protestant clergyman) engaged in homosexual acts. A scandal erupted over the dubious tactics of the operation when they became public, and it continued to simmer for years. In 1921 a Senate investigation, dominated by Republicans, openly chastised Roosevelt for his part in the action.[8]

In the meantime, Roosevelt was experiencing a personal crisis that was even more threatening to his future. Almost from the moment he arrived in Washington in 1913, he was a fixture in the city's active social life—a lively, handsome, gregarious presence at innumerable dinners, dances, and receptions. In the process, he often found himself at odds with his wife, to whom social events were seldom less than an ordeal. Eleanor often stayed home with the children when Franklin went out. At times, she left parties early and alone. Perhaps in part as a result of his wife's painful reserve, Franklin found himself drawn to the poised, attractive, outgoing young woman Eleanor had hired as her social secretary: Lucy Mercer. Eventually, they formed a romantic relationship, which blossomed during the summer months when Eleanor and the children were at the family's summer home on Campobello Island, while Franklin stayed behind in Washington. The relationship continued until Eleanor discovered it late in 1918, when she found some letters between her husband and her secretary. It was a decisive moment in their marriage. Aware that a divorce would end his political career (and, his mother threatened, her financial support for him), Franklin declined Eleanor's offer of a divorce and promised to end all relations with Lucy Mercer (a promise he later broke). Eleanor was deeply wounded, withdrew from any real intimacy with her husband, and began to build her own, independent public career. Their marriage survived on the basis of shared public commitments and residual respect and affection. But from 1918 on, they lived increasingly separate lives. Roosevelt's relationship with his wife, like his relationship with many others, became characterized by surface charm, emotional distance, and elaborate patterns of deception.[9]

Despite the occasional travails of his Washington experience, Roosevelt emerged from his eight years in the Navy Department with a significantly enhanced reputation. Theodore Roosevelt had died in 1919, an event that made Franklin's own famous name especially appealing to national Democratic leaders. In 1920 he secured the Democratic Party's nomination for vice president on the ill-fated ticket headed by Ohio governor James M. Cox. Roosevelt campaigned energetically and at times rashly. Once, defending the League of Nations, he falsely claimed that he had written the constitution of Haiti, and thus had that nation's vote "in his pocket." But he emerged from the experience with little of the blame for the Democrats' crushing defeat and with many new friends among party leaders.[10]

In 1921 Roosevelt returned to private life for the first time since his election to the New York State Senate eleven years earlier. He was now a thirty-six-year-old man with a national reputation and an apparently limitless future. His public image was that of an attractive and articulate young politician with no reputation for strong commitments. Unlike his cousin Theodore, who had always been distinguished by the passion with which he held and promoted his convictions, Franklin had an actual aversion to deep ideological beliefs; throughout his life he sought politically pragmatic routes through the thickets of dogma surrounding him. But he was not wholly without conviction. From Theodore Roosevelt, his first political idol, he had derived a lasting commitment to a highly nationalistic view of government—a belief that Washington had an important role to play in the life of the nation, and that America had a great destiny in the world. From Woodrow Wilson, the president he had served, he drew a belief in internationalism. But perhaps equally important, he also drew an acute sense of the political dangers of moving too quickly, as he believed Wilson had tried to do, toward thrusting the United States into cooperative relationships with other nations. From the progressive battles of the early twentieth century that he had observed but rarely joined in his youth, he acquired a general sense that in the modern industrial world there were dangerous sources of instability and great imbalances of power, and that concerted public action was necessary to address the problems they caused. But he did not identify himself clearly with any one faction within the highly eclectic array of progressive reformers. In later years, he would continue to draw from many different, even incompatible, advisers and clusters of belief.[11]

Once back in New York, he became a vice president of a bonding company and formed a legal partnership, intending all the while to focus primarily on politics. In August 1921, however, a personal disaster seemed to shatter all his hopes. He joined his family at their summer home on Campobello Island several weeks after visiting a Boy Scout camp outside New York, where he may have been exposed to the poliomyelitis virus. A few days after his arrival, he fell ill.[12]

The disease appeared first as a fever after a strenuous morning of outdoor activity with his children. Within days, he had lost the use of both his legs and was in excruciating pain. Months later, after a belated diagnosis of the disease as polio, his doctors told him that he would never walk again. Roosevelt refused to believe them, and he spent much of the next seven years in a futile search for a cure. He tried innumerable forms of therapy, some medically respectable and others indistinguishable from quackery. At times he seemed determined simply to will himself to walk—as in his repeated, and always unsuccessful, efforts to carry himself on crutches to the end of the long driveway of his family home in Hyde Park.[13]

Although Eleanor Roosevelt had nursed her husband devotedly through the first traumatic months of his illness, the polio ultimately increased their estrangement. She sided with her husband and Louis Howe in support of Franklin's determination to return to politics, a course his mother bitterly opposed. Sara wanted him to retire to Hyde Park and live as her husband had lived—that is, as an invalid country gentleman. But Franklin's struggle for recovery made him more self-centered than ever. Confined for the first time to his home, he engaged in elaborate strategies to protect himself from the competing demands of his family, to pit them against one another, and, finally, to distance himself from them all.[14]

For several years Roosevelt spent months at a time away from home. During the winters, he lived on a houseboat in Florida, hoping that the sun and fresh air would help revive his legs. He became particularly attached to the spa-like baths he discovered in Warm Springs, Georgia, and he spent much of his own money buying an old resort hotel and converting it into a center for polio patients. There he became the ebullient leader of dispirited groups of men, women, and children, exhorting them to work toward recovery, as he had done, and providing (if unintentionally) an example of how the power of bravado and denial had helped someone who could not regain the use of his legs but who could gain some control of his life.

Roosevelt became accustomed, as he would remain for the rest of his life, to building around himself a protective (and frequently changing) circle of friends, aides, and flatterers who helped him sustain the atmosphere of artificial gaiety and lighthearted banter in which he had always felt most comfortable. In 1920, Marguerite "Missy" LeHand became his personal secretary. She became a constant daily presence in his life, as an aide, a companion, and (when Franklin and Eleanor were apart, as they often were) a hostess. In some senses, she also became a surrogate wife. She was almost certainly in love with him. He was heavily dependent on her, but it is not likely he was romantically attracted. Eleanor Roosevelt may have felt some jealousy toward Missy's increasingly central role in her husband's life, but if so, she never revealed it. Instead, she cultivated a close relationship of her own with LeHand, whose devotion to Franklin made it easier for Eleanor to continue pursuing her own career.

Roosevelt's long search for a cure for polio inevitably ended in failure. Eventually, he became at least partially reconciled to his paralysis, and he learned to disguise it for public purposes by wearing heavy leg braces; supporting himself, first with crutches and later with a cane and the arm of a companion; and using his hips to swing his inert legs forward. He tried to compensate for the discomfort his disability might create in those around him with an aggressively cheerful countenance. As he labored to move from room to room, and while aides lifted him in and out of cars and trains, he smiled broadly, waved cheerfully, chattered, and told jokes—anything to distract others from his physical limitations. Most of his public appearances were carefully staged to hide his laborious movements. He was often seen standing, but only rarely "walking." When he traveled by train, he almost always spoke from the rear platform while supported by a reinforced podium. When he moved about by automobile, he spoke to crowds from the back seat of an open car or used specially constructed ramps to have himself driven as close to podiums as possible. He painted his steel braces black and had his trousers cut long to obscure them from the public. Later, when he was president, White House aides ensured that no one ever photographed him in a way that would reveal his disability. Of all the thousands of photographs of him in the Roosevelt Library in Hyde Park, only a handful—taken privately by relatives—show him sitting in a wheelchair.

So effective was this deception (and so cooperative was the press in preserving it) that few Americans knew that Roosevelt could not walk. On the contrary, most believed that he had suffered, struggled, and recovered from his affliction—much as Theodore Roosevelt had rebuilt himself from a frail, asthmatic child into a husky, energetic adult. Prior to contracting polio, Franklin had been a slight and slender man—charming and attractive, but, in appearance at least, not robust in the way Theodore had seemed. Franklin's strenuous efforts to strengthen his upper body so that he could move himself without his legs gave him a new appearance of physical power, for he developed broad shoulders, a heavily muscled chest, and a ramrod-straight posture. In drawings and political cartoons, he was often portrayed as a strong, muscular man, and he was frequently shown standing, running, leaping, even boxing. These were all testaments to his success in conveying an image of energy and mobility.

Roosevelt rarely talked about his own feelings, least of all about the impact his paralysis had on him. But contracting polio was clearly one of the most important events of his life. His determination to hide his condition from those around him probably strengthened what was already his natural inclination to dissemble, to hide behind an aggressive public geniality, and to reveal as little about himself as possible. Eleanor Roosevelt later claimed that polio also gave him patience and increased his understanding of "what suffering meant." Whatever else it did, the ordeal made him more serious and determined, and he gradually transferred his steely new resolve away from his efforts to walk and toward an attempt to resume a public career.[15]

During much of the 1920s, Roosevelt maintained his ties to politics largely through correspondence, most of it orchestrated by Howe, and through the increasingly public activities of Eleanor. He developed a close political relationship, although never a personal one, with Al Smith, the Tammany-supported governor of New York. He also forged ties to other groups in the Democratic Party and presented himself as a bridge between its two bitterly divided wings: one represented by Smith, who attracted largely eastern, urban, Catholic, and ethnic voters; the other represented by William Jennings Bryan and William G. McAdoo, whose followers were largely southern, western, rural, and Protestant. Only by uniting these warring factions, Roosevelt believed, could the Democrats hope to challenge the dominance of national politics that Republicans had sustained since 1896—a dominance broken only by Woodrow Wilson's triumphs over divided opposition in 1912 and 1916.[16]

In 1924 Roosevelt attended the disastrous Democratic National Convention, during which the party's two great factions did battle for 103 ballots before spurning both Smith and McAdoo and nominating the pallid and uncontroversial John W. Davis, a corporate lawyer. Before that dreary battle, a grim-faced Roosevelt dragged himself laboriously to the podium on crutches and placed Smith's name in nomination. He made no further public appearances until 1928, when he again nominated Smith for president at the national convention, this time "walking" to the podium without crutches, one hand holding a cane and the other clutching his son's arm. It was an important personal triumph that helped lay to rest public doubts about his health. It also signaled his readiness to resume an active political career, which he did more quickly than even he had expected. After months of resisting pressure from Smith and other party leaders to run for governor of New York, he finally agreed to be a candidate in 1928. He campaigned energetically and buoyantly, continuing to dispel rumors of incapacity. Smith lost his home state to Herbert Hoover in the presidential contest by 100,000 votes, but Roosevelt defeated the Republican gubernatorial candidate, Albert Ottinger, by a narrow margin.[17]

His four years as governor coincided with the first three and a half years of the Great Depression. More quickly than President Hoover and most Democratic leaders, he concluded that the economy would not recover on its own, stating, "there is a duty on the part of government to do something about this." Hoover, he argued, "has shown an extraordinary lack of leadership." There was relatively little a state government could do to fight a national, and eventually international, depression, but Roosevelt pushed for a series of modest reforms that, if nothing else, reinforced his image as an energetic progressive. He enacted measures to develop public electric power, lower utilities rates, and reduce the tax burden on New York farmers. Later, he created a state agency to provide relief to the unemployed and began calling for national unemployment insurance and other government programs to assist the jobless. But he was careful not to seem reckless or radical. He criticized Hoover for failing to balance the budget, and he even denounced the Republican administration at times for intruding the government too far into the life of the economy.[18]

From the moment of his landslide reelection to a second two-year term as governor of New York in 1930, he was the obvious front-runner for the 1932 Democratic presidential nomination. With the help of Howe and James A. Farley, a talented New York political organizer who had helped orchestrate Roosevelt's two gubernatorial campaigns, he accumulated pledges from delegates throughout the country, particularly in the South and West, where antipathy to Smith, Roosevelt's chief rival for the nomination, was strong. Even so, he approached the Democratic National Convention far from certain of nomination. Smith had defeated him in the Massachusetts primary, and House Speaker John Nance Garner of Texas had won the California primary. Their delegate strength, when combined with that of other candidates and favorite sons, denied Roosevelt through three ballots the two-thirds vote the Democratic Party then required for nomination. But on the fourth ballot Garner released his delegates (after Roosevelt promised him the vice presidential nomination), and the votes from Texas gave Roosevelt the margin he needed. The following day, he broke with tradition by flying to Chicago, becoming the first major-party candidate to travel by airplane and the first ever to appear personally before a convention to accept its nomination. In his speech to the delegates, he pledged "a new deal for the American people." Within weeks, the phrase became a widely accepted label for his as-yet unspecified program.[19]

His task in the fall campaign was a relatively simple one: avoid doing anything to alarm the electorate while allowing Hoover's enormous unpopularity to drive voters to the Democrats. Roosevelt traveled extensively, giving speeches filled with sunny generalities. He was unfailingly genial and ebullient. He continued to criticize Hoover for failing to balance the budget and for expanding the bureaucracy, but he only occasionally gave indications of his own vaguely progressive agenda. In the most important speech of the campaign, at the Commonwealth Club in San Francisco, he outlined in broad terms a new set of government responsibilities: providing "enlightened administration" to help the economy revive, distributing "wealth and products more equitably," and giving "everyone an avenue to possess himself of a portion of that plenty sufficient for his needs, through his own work."[20]

The presidential campaign brought together those who had guided Roosevelt's career in the past and those who would shape his presidency thereafter. Louis Howe and James Farley remained his principal political strategists. Eleanor Roosevelt continued to serve as a surrogate for her husband, even while she was developing an important reputation of her own. But 1932 also brought Roosevelt into contact with new aides and advisers, perhaps most notably a group of academics dubbed the "brain trust" by reporters. Chief among them were three Columbia University economists—Raymond Moley, Adolf A. Berle Jr., and Rexford G. Tugwell—who helped write his campaign speeches, including the Commonwealth Club address.

More important, they began developing ideas for his presidency based on their own growing belief in the need for a rational plan for American economic life.[21]

Roosevelt found himself particularly attracted to the "brain trust" vision of a harmonious economy, a vision inspired in large part by the American experience of mobilization for World War I. Like many members of his generation, he viewed the experiments in industrial organization during the war years as possible models for a peacetime economic order. He was interested in creating a new "cooperative commonwealth" in which business, labor, and government would work together to stabilize the economy. He was also attracted to the more statist ideas of those who, like Tugwell, believed in a more direct form of government economic planning. But proponents of "harmony" and planning were not the only people who had his ear. Roosevelt listened to a broad and eclectic group of advisers and exhorters from throughout the Democratic Party, including inveterate antimonopolists of the South and West, who urged him to look skeptically at the size and influence of great corporations; those who had struggled throughout the 1920s to bring the federal government into the development of hydroelectric power, so as to challenge the private utilities and bring down prices; advocates of public works and state investment in infrastructure, who sought to use government to spur the economic development of underdeveloped regions; agrarian reformers, who had spent a decade promoting plans for stabilizing farm prices (embodied in the McNary-Haugen bills that Congress had twice passed and Calvin Coolidge had twice vetoed in the 1920s); labor leaders eager for the protection of unions; and social workers and welfare strategists of his own state (of whom his wife was one), who argued strenuously for an expanded federal role in relief and social insurance.[22]

Among other significant figures who moved into his orbit as he campaigned for the presidency were Felix Frankfurter, the brilliant Harvard Law School professor and frequent critic of monopoly, whose large network of talented students ultimately populated many New Deal agencies; Henry A. Wallace, the visionary Iowa reformer who would become Roosevelt's secretary of agriculture; Harry Hopkins, the impassioned social worker and (at least at first) close friend of Eleanor Roosevelt, who became the New Deal's "minister of relief" and eventually the president's closest advisor; Frances Perkins, a reformer who served as Roosevelt's industrial commissioner in New York and later as secretary of labor during his presidency, and was the first woman ever to serve in the Cabinet; and Jesse Jones, the conservative Texas banker and champion of government investment in infrastructure projects, whom Roosevelt retained as director of the Reconstruction

Finance Corporation and later named secretary of commerce. Roosevelt never lacked for talented aides and advisers; his challenge was to mediate among their diverse and often conflicting views.[23]

Roosevelt won the presidency handily, with 57 percent of the popular vote to Hoover's 40 percent, and with 472 electoral votes to Hoover's 59. Democrats also won solid control of both houses of Congress. Many observers interpreted the results less as a mandate for Roosevelt, whose plans remained largely unknown to the public, than as a repudiation of Hoover. There were also skeptics who shared the columnist Walter Lippmann's famously dismissive view of Roosevelt as "a pleasant man who, without any important qualifications for the office, would very much like to be president."[24]

In the four months between his victory and his inauguration, Roosevelt did little to dispel those doubts. The Depression worsened considerably that winter and reached its nadir in the first months of 1933. President Hoover, conservative Democrats, and leading business figures all urged the president-elect to restore confidence by pledging himself to fiscal and monetary conservatism. Roosevelt ignored their advice and continued to offer few clues regarding his own plans. The most dramatic event of his "interregnum" was an assassination attempt in Miami a few weeks before his inauguration. Roosevelt, the shooter's target, was not injured, but Anton Cermak, the mayor of Chicago, was killed. The president-elect responded to the incident with the same unruffled calm he had displayed since the election.[25]

Several weeks before the 1933 presidential inauguration, the cartoonist Peter Arno had prepared a cover illustration for the *New Yorker* magazine. It portrayed Franklin Roosevelt and Herbert Hoover riding together in an open car, wearing top hats, and following the traditional route from the White House to the Capitol for the swearing-in ceremony. Gaping crowds lined the route. Arno drew Hoover slumped in his seat, glum, unsmiling, peering sideways—somewhat suspiciously—at his successor. Roosevelt was smiling broadly, head raised, looking ebulliently at the crowds. In the aftermath of the Miami shooting, the *New Yorker* decided not to run the cover. But on Inauguration Day, March 4, 1933, photographers captured the actual scene of the ride to the Capitol, an image uncannily similar to the one Arno had imagined weeks before: Hoover, the repudiated president, sour and silent, as if aware that after years at the center of public life he faced thirty years of marginalization and near oblivion; and Franklin Roosevelt, beaming, insouciant, and inscrutable, his head thrust high, riding toward his rendezvous with destiny.[26]

C

Roosevelt assumed the presidency at a moment of great crisis for the nation. Unemployment had reached 24 percent, and many more were underemployed or underpaid and unable to support themselves or their families. The agricultural economy was mired in a deep depression that had long preceded 1929. Industrial production had fallen dramatically, and new capital investment had almost evaporated. The gross national product (GNP) had dropped by over 30 percent since 1929. But the most immediate task facing the new president was the unraveling of the banking system, which had become virtually paralyzed as a widening panic drained many banks of their reserves. The governor of Michigan had ordered all the banks in his state closed in mid-February, and by the beginning of March almost every state in the nation had placed restrictions on banking activity.[27]

The banking crisis provided the ominous backdrop both for Roosevelt's inauguration and for his first days in office. His inaugural address offered words of assurance ("The only thing we have to fear is fear itself"), stern warnings ("The rulers of the exchange of mankind's goods have failed through their own stubbornness and their own incompetence....The money changers have fled from their high seats in the temple of our civilization"), and bold promises ("action, and action now"). It was less a diagnosis of the national condition than a direct response to the banking crisis itself, and his first weeks in office were devoted largely to solving that crisis. On his first full day in office, March 6, 1933, he ordered every bank in the nation closed—a "bank holiday," as he euphemistically described it. Three days later, Congress met in special session to consider an emergency banking bill, drafted so hastily (mostly by holdovers from the Hoover administration) that members did not even receive printed copies of it. Both houses passed it, and the president signed it the same day. Stronger banks quickly reopened with promises of government assistance; weaker ones remained closed until Treasury Department examiners could assure their viability. This was a modest and essentially conservative step, but it was enough to stop the panic. Nearly three-quarters of the nation's banks reopened within three days of the measure's passage.[28]

A few days later, Roosevelt delivered the first of his avuncular "fireside chats" over national radio, during which he explained the provisions of the banking bill in simple terms and offered comforting assurances that "it is safer to keep your money in a reopened bank than it is to keep it under your mattress." The president continued to use radio throughout his administration—he was the first national leader whose voice became a part of the country's everyday life. Three months later, Congress passed the Glass-Steagall Banking Act, which separated commercial banks from investment banks, gave the government authority to curb irresponsible speculation by banks, and created the Federal Deposit Insurance Corporation, which guaranteed individual bank deposits. Combined with the 1935 Banking Act, which strengthened the provisions of the original Glass-Steagall Act, it was perhaps the most important banking legislation of the twentieth century.[29]

But not all of Roosevelt's early decisions contributed to stability or recovery. This was largely because the New Dealers had only vague ideas of what had caused the crisis, and thus had no clear idea of how to fix it. Some believed the Depression was a result of overproduction, which had driven down prices and launched the spiraling deflation.

Others argued that the problem was underconsumption and the inadequate incomes of working people, which created weak markets for consumer goods. Some believed that the problem was the composition of the currency, others that it was a lack of "business confidence." Virtually no one yet accepted what became the Keynesian ideas that promoted aggressive public spending to generate economic activity during a recession.[30]

Roosevelt's first response to these conflicting pressures was a relatively conservative one. He had promised during his 1932 campaign that he would end the deficits that had plagued the Hoover administration, and one of his first acts in 1933 was to propose legislation cutting government salaries, veterans' benefits, and other federal budgets. Both Houses passed the Economy Act within days, despite protests from some progressives who argued correctly that the measure would add to the deflationary pressures on the economy. Roosevelt continued to believe in a balanced budget throughout his presidency, but he only occasionally pursued that goal, discovering when he tried that it usually did more harm than good.[31]

In time-honored fashion, Roosevelt also tinkered with the currency. First he sabotaged an international economic conference that was meeting in London to stabilize world currencies. He had sent his secretary of state, Cordell Hull, and his economic adviser, Raymond Moley, to the meeting, having urged them to try to restore the international gold standard, from which Britain had recently retreated. But a few days later, having changed his mind about the importance of the gold standard, he abruptly repudiated his earlier instructions and sent a telegram from Washington saying that the United States would not be bound by the decisions of the conference. The "bombshell message," as his statement came to be known, brought the London Economic Conference to an immediate end. In mid-April, Roosevelt issued an executive order repudiating the centrality of the gold standard. Both before and after the April decision, the administration began experimenting in various ways with manipulating the value of the dollar—first by making substantial purchases of gold and silver, and later by establishing a new, fixed standard for the dollar, while reducing its gold content substantially. This resort to a government-managed currency—to a dollar whose value could be raised or lowered by government policy—helped create an important precedent for future economic policies. But it did not have much immediate impact on the depressed economy.[32]

Over the next three months, which came to be known as the "Hundred Days," Roosevelt won passage of a series of bills that began to transform the role of the federal government in the workings of the nation's economy. In the process, he revealed clearly for the first time how eclectic his ideas were and how pragmatically he approached the crisis he had inherited.

The farm economy had been in something like a depression since the mid-1920s. In an age when agriculture played a larger role in the nation's economy than it later would, and when farmers were a more numerous and more important political force than they would later become, the agrarian crisis was a matter of great urgency to Roosevelt's administration. Farmers were facing excess production and falling prices. A severe drought that began in 1932 led to what became known as the "Dust Bowl"— a broad swath of devastated western farmland that forced hundreds of thousand of people off their land—which worsened the agricultural economy even further. The Agricultural Adjustment Act, a comprehensive farm bill that Roosevelt signed in May 1933, attempted to address these problems. It set out to end the chronic agricultural overproduction and to lift inadequate prices by limiting production and subsidizing farmers.

The Agricultural Adjustment Administration (AAA), which the legislation created, identified seven basic commodities (wheat, cotton, corn, hogs, rice, tobacco, and dairy products) and paid farmers to take acreage out of production. The AAA also guaranteed them a fair price for the goods they did produce. There were additional provisions for preventing excess concentration and monopoly in the agricultural economy and for protecting small farmers, tenants, and sharecroppers. But much of the administration of the program fell into the hands of the American Farm Bureau Federation, which represented mostly commercial farmers. Unsurprisingly, therefore, the AAA tended to ignore the provisions that were supposed to help small farmers, and instead generally favored large producers. Farm income rose by almost 50 percent in the next three years, and prices rose significantly for most major commodities. But the dispossession of small farmers, tenants, and sharecroppers continued and even accelerated. The program was particularly hard on African Americans, who formed a large proportion of the landless farmers in the South and had less political leverage than their white counterparts. The workings of the AAA became part of the process that drove many farmers off the land and into towns and cities.[33]

The New Deal experimented with a series of other programs designed to help these marginal farmers, including the Resettlement Administration, established in 1935, and the Farm Security Administration, created in 1937, but the movement of the agricultural economy toward large-scale commercial farming continued inexorably. In 1936 the Supreme Court invalidated the original Agricultural Adjustment Act, declaring that Congress had no authority to compel individual farmers to reduce their acreage. The Farm Bureau mobilized quickly to rewrite the law to answer the Court's objections, and their efforts preserved the bill's major provisions in slightly altered form through the Soil Conservation and Domestic Allotment Act of 1936 and the Agricultural Adjustment Act of 1938. Federal support for farmers continued, in similar if diminished form, into the twenty-first century.[34]

Roosevelt's second major challenge during the "Hundred Days" was the health of the industrial economy. Members of the U.S. Chamber of Commerce, the president of General Electric, Gerard Swope, and other leading businessmen and industrialists had been urging the government to suspend the antitrust laws and allow corporations to work together to stabilize prices and production. The "Swope Plan" proposed a cooperative "associationalism" among firms, policed in some modest way by the government. Hoover had rejected the idea, but Roosevelt revived it—although not exactly as the industrialists had hoped. In June 1933 he introduced a proposal that built on the private-sector proposals but added a strong role for the government. The result was the National Industrial Recovery Act (NIRA), enacted later that month. Roosevelt called it "the most important and far-reaching legislation ever enacted by the American Congress." The NIRA established a National Recovery Administration (NRA), headed by the flamboyant Hugh Johnson, a retired general who had directed the selective service system during World War I. Its most important task was persuading industrialists in the major industries to join together under "code authorities" through which industries would establish price floors, production restrictions, and employment standards to check deflation and restore prosperity. The codes, which could be enforced through governmental sanctions, provided exemptions from antitrust laws and gave the agreements the force of law. For businesses too small to participate in the industrial codes, Johnson created a largely voluntary (and mostly unenforceable) "blanket code" that proposed standards for smaller businesses. It established a minimum wage of 30 to 40 cents an hour, a maximum workweek of 35 to 40 hours, and the abolition of child labor.[35]

The NRA swung into action quickly and impressively. Within weeks, almost every major industry had drawn up a code and had agreed to abide by its provisions; the energetic Johnson quickly approved them. He was particularly successful in creating public excitement about the new program and its iconography. The agency's famous symbol, the Blue Eagle, soon appeared in shop windows and emblazoned on banners carried in "Blue Eagle" rallies (one of which, in New York, was the largest parade in the city's history—larger than the great celebration that had greeted Charles Lindbergh on his return from Paris nearly a decade before). Thousands of schoolchildren in

San Francisco celebrated the NRA by assembling on a playing field in the shape of an eagle for photographers. The owner of the Philadelphia professional football team renamed it the "Eagles" in honor of the agency.[36]

But the initial enthusiasm could not long disguise the fundamental problems at the heart of the experiment. Administratively unprepared for the enormity of its task, the agency floundered as it tried to enforce the codes, many of which were hastily and poorly constructed, and almost all of which were dominated by the largest producers. As a result, the codes served some large corporations reasonably well. Big firms could keep their prices up without having to fear being undercut by smaller competitors. They often raised prices artificially to levels higher than the market could sustain. Small businesses, however, were usually unable to compete with larger firms *unless* they undercut them in price. Forcing small businesses to charge the same as large ones, which the codes tried to do, often meant robbing them of their only access to the market. Despite the NIRA's Section 7(a), which guaranteed workers the right to organize and bargain collectively, the agency permitted labor virtually no role at all in setting their guidelines. Workers organized, but they lacked any effective enforcement mechanism and companies continued to refuse to bargain with them. The biggest problem of the NRA, however, was the basic assumption behind it. The NRA catered to industry fears of overproduction and thus became a vehicle that encouraged manufacturers to lower production, reduce wages, and increase prices at a time when the economy needed exactly the opposite. Industrial production actually declined significantly in the first year of the NRA's existence.[37]

By early 1934, the failure of the NRA was already becoming clear. After an external review board chaired by Clarence Darrow charged that the agency was dominated by big business and was encouraging monopoly, Roosevelt pressured Hugh Johnson to resign. But Johnson's successors made little progress in solving the NRA's problem. In May 1935 a case came before the Supreme Court charging NRA code violations by the Schechter brothers, who operated a wholesale poultry business in Brooklyn, New York. The Schechters' attorneys argued that the poultry company was not engaged in "interstate commerce" and therefore lay outside of federal control. The Supreme Court agreed. It also ruled that Congress had unconstitutionally delegated legislative powers to the president in creating the NRA codes themselves. Alarmed by the decision, the president charged that the Court had adopted a "horse-and-buggy" interpretation of the Constitution. He was rightly concerned, for the Court's narrow construction of the interstate commerce clause and strict view of the limits on executive power called many other New

Deal measures into question. Even so, the nullification of the NRA itself rescued the president from a failed experiment—and one that, unlike the AAA, he made no serious attempt to revive.[38]

The AAA and the NRA—with their visions of government, labor, and capitalism working together to create an ordered economic world—reflected only one of the many approaches Roosevelt and the New Dealers adopted in an effort to defeat the Depression. Early in his presidency, Roosevelt also became interested in challenging the power of large industrial combinations and monopolies. He took a particular interest in the price of electricity, which Roosevelt believed was artificially high because of monopoly control. He settled on the idea of "yardsticks," experiments in government production of power that might reveal the true cost of electricity, and thus allow the government to compete with private producers and force them to lower prices. The most prominent of these experiments was the Tennessee Valley Authority (TVA), approved by Congress in May 1933. Progressives had been arguing for years that the government should complete a large dam and hydroelectric project at Muscle Shoals, Alabama, that had been left unfinished after World War I. The TVA not only revived the Muscle Shoals project, which became an important source of electricity for the region; it also built a network of other dams and facilities to generate power, reduce flooding, provide irrigation, and raise the incomes of the residents of the broad area that became part of the experiment. The TVA produced electricity priced at roughly half of what private companies had been charging, an achievement that helped lower electricity prices across much of the country. It also contributed to the creation in 1935 of the Rural Electrification Administration (REA), which used government funds to extend access to electricity into remote rural areas that power companies had considered too expensive to serve. Little came of the TVA's vaguely Utopian images of a great transformation of the region into a planned and ordered community. But it was an important first step in the New Deal's strong commitment to public works and regional development, which continued through Roosevelt's presidency.[39]

At the same time, Roosevelt proposed new regulations for the financial sector and won passage of the Securities Act of 1933, which strengthened the regulation of securities and led to the creation of the Securities and Exchange Commission (SEC) in June 1934. The SEC was the successor to a series of existing regulatory measures enacted in the early twentieth century to control the behaviors of commercial banks and corporations. It extended those regulations to the workings of Wall Street and required traders to reveal information that would allow investors to make informed decisions.[40]

For the millions of unemployed Americans, the most important actions of the new government were the New Deal's efforts to provide relief to the jobless. The Federal Emergency Relief Administration (FERA), enacted in May 1933, used $500 million of federal funds to shore up state and local relief agencies that had become overwhelmed by demand. But Roosevelt and Hopkins were uneasy with the FERA. They feared what they believed were the debilitating effects of "the dole." Hopkins, looking at the results of the FERA in 1933, said, "I don't think anybody can go on year after year, month after month, accepting relief without affecting his character in some way unfavorably. It is probably going to undermine the independence of hundreds of thousands of families.... I look upon this as a great national disaster." Roosevelt agreed, saying, "I do not want to think that it is the destiny of any American to remain permanently on the relief rolls." As a result, future relief measures focused on creating jobs.[41]

The Civilian Conservation Corps (CCC), created in the first weeks of Roosevelt's presidency, better reflected Roosevelt and Hopkins's views of relief. It provided jobs for over a million young, unemployed men, many of them from cities, to work in national parks and forests. (As with many New Deal programs, African Americans were allowed to participate, but only in segregated units and often with lower pay scales.) The CCC reflected the president's belief in the value of the countryside and in the importance of what his cousin Theodore Roosevelt had called the "strenuous life." A few months later, Congress authorized the Civil Works Administration (CWA), a federally managed jobs program that put over 4 million people to work on construction projects between November 1933 and April 1934.[42]

It was not only the unemployed that attracted the New Deal's attention. The government also created new protections for home and land owners. The Farm Credit Administration refinanced 20 percent of all farm mortgages in its first two years. The Frazier-Lemke Farm Bankruptcy Act of 1933 enabled some farmers to regain their land even after foreclosure. The 1933 Home Owners' Loan Act, which created the Home Owners' Loan Corporation (HOLC), helped homeowners refinance over a million mortgages and avoid foreclosures. The National Housing Act of 1934 created the Federal Housing Administration (FHA), which regulated interest rates, insured mortgages, and thus increased access to housing.[43]

The first hundred days of Roosevelt's presidency were impressive, important, and, to many Americans, baffling. The achievements fit no clear pattern and reflected no firm principles. But Roosevelt nevertheless presented himself to the world as a beacon of confidence and optimism.

In the panicked environment in which he entered office, that alone was a significant achievement. The firm, confident voice, the smiling optimism, the cock of the head, the uptilted cigarette holder, the beaming smile—all helped many desperate people believe that there was hope in their leadership, that the head of their nation was not just a bureaucrat but a symbol of their highest aspirations. Roosevelt's own most important commitment was always to what he called the "spirit of persistent experimentation." Critics and admirers alike argued that the New Deal reflected nothing but pragmatic responses to critical problems, that it was, as the historian Richard Hofstadter once wrote, little more than a "chaos of experimentation." "To look upon these programs as the result of a unified plan," Roosevelt's one-time advisor Raymond Moley wrote in a sour memoir published after his falling out with the president, "was to believe that the accumulation of stuffed snakes, baseball pictures, school flags, old tennis shoes, carpenter's tools, geometry books, and chemistry sets in a boy's bedroom could have been put there by an interior decorator." But Roosevelt was not troubled by the seeming chaos of his policies, and he continued to search for new and better approaches to the crisis. "Take a method and try it," he liked to say. "If it fails, admit it frankly and try another. But above all, try something."[44]

By the end of 1933, although the free fall of the economy had largely ended, real recovery had not yet begun. The GNP, which had fallen by a staggering 13.4 percent in 1932, fell by only 2.1 percent in 1933. Unemployment, which had grown by 7.7 percent in 1932, grew by only 1.3 percent in 1933. Roosevelt's popularity remained strong, but he understood that, for all his successes, he had not yet found a secure road to recovery. Over the next year, he began searching for new approaches even while some of his early experiments foundered.

Spurring him on was a growing and significant opposition. Some of it came from the traditional right: industrialists, bankers, investors, and other mostly wealthy conservatives. A group of such people, led by the du Pont family (owners of the great chemical company that bore their name) established the Liberty League in 1934. They railed against the "dictatorial" tactics of the New Deal and the intrusion of government into capitalist institutions, and they reflected the growing hatred of Roosevelt among many wealthy elites, especially in the Northeast. More significant—and more dangerous to Roosevelt's political future—were growing populist protests from people who had once supported him. Local dissident movements sprang up across the country, including in Wisconsin, Minnesota, Iowa, California, Texas, Oregon, and other states. Senator Huey Long of Louisiana, the "radio priest" Father Charles Coughlin, and the old-age pension champion Dr. Francis Townsend all formed national movements that proposed dramatic new answers to the problems of the economy. Long proposed a radical redistribution of wealth and launched a national "Share Our Wealth Society." Coughlin argued for an inflation of the currency and the nationalization of banks, and he used his network radio program to create an organization he called the National Union for Social Justice. Townsend's "Old-Age Revolving Pension Plan" proposed federal pensions for the elderly, both to improve their lives and to pump new money into the economy. They all hoped that their movements might help them to elect a new president more sympathetic to their goals in 1936, or that they might at least put pressure on the government to take their demands more seriously.

When Long was assassinated in late 1935, some of his followers joined Coughlin and Townsend in launching the new Union Party, which ultimately presented a weak third-party presidential candidate in 1936.[45]

Disappointment and impatience with Roosevelt were not restricted to wealthy conservatives and populist dissidents. He also faced growing disillusionment from the vast pool of the unemployed, and even from some members of his own administration, who felt he was ineffectively improvising and was in danger of failing. "It simply has to be admitted," his aide Rexford Tugwell wrote years later of the New Deal in 1934, "that Roosevelt was not yet certain what direction he ought to take." Although the economy finally showed significant growth in 1934—an almost 10 percent rise in GNP and an almost 3 percent decline in unemployment—to many Americans the New Deal seemed to have run out of ideas. After the great flurry of activity in 1933, the relatively modest legislative achievements of 1934 did little to reassure an increasingly troubled public. Roosevelt was acutely aware of these challenges to his leadership, and he responded aggressively with a wave of new initiatives that came to be known as the "Second New Deal." This period of activity became, if anything, more ambitious and more important than the Hundred Days.[46]

With unemployment still very high (just under 22 percent at the end of 1934), Roosevelt and Hopkins proposed a new jobs program that was much larger than any previous national effort. The Works Progress Administration (WPA) set out to create jobs for as many people as possible, and with a budget of $8 billion (a sum larger than total peacetime federal budgets prior to 1933) it was able to hire three million people in its first year and a total of over eight million during its eight-year existence. Hopkins's first priority was to provide immediate assistance to the unemployed, and he spent the money allotted to him lavishly, rapidly, and with considerable creativity. The WPA built hospitals, schools, airports, theaters, roads, hotels in national parks, monuments, post offices, and other federal buildings all over the country. It also created some of the most imaginative government projects in American history. The Federal Theater Project hired actors, directors, playwrights, and other unemployed theater people to write and produce plays, skits, and revues. The Federal Arts Project recruited unemployed artists and put them to work creating, among other things, public art. The Federal Writers' Project produced state and city guidebooks and collected oral histories from ordinary men and women, including former slaves. Most of all, the WPA helped desperately needy people find jobs, and it pumped much-needed funds into the economy. It raised popular expectations of government and helped legitimize the idea of public assistance to the poor. But the WPA did not become a model for a lasting federal role in social welfare. Congress abolished it in 1943, after the war had essentially eliminated unemployment. Federal jobs programs have been rare and modest in the years since.[47]

Among the New Deal achievements that did become important and lasting parts of the American welfare state were the programs of government assistance created by the most important piece of social legislation in American history, the Social Security Act of 1935. The act had its roots in European social welfare programs developed over the previous half century, in the aspirations of social workers and settlement houses in the Progressive Era, and in state-level programs that Roosevelt had studied while he was governor of New York. Some of his progressive colleagues from New York joined a large group of other social activists and social scientists to propose an extraordinary piece of legislation. The Social Security Act set up several important programs, including unemployment compensation (funded by employers) and old-age pensions (funded by a Social Security tax paid jointly by employers and employees). It also provided assistance to the disabled (primarily the blind) and the elderly poor (people presumably too old to work). And it established Aid to Dependent Children (later called Aid to Families with Dependent Children, or AFDC), which created the model for what most Americans considered "welfare" for over sixty years. Unemployment insurance and old-age pensions had little difficulty achieving political legitimacy, because the benefits they provided could be understood as "insurance" rather than welfare; the programs allowed recipients to feel that they had earned or paid for their support. Social insurance remained popular despite the deflationary effects of the Social Security pension tax in its first years, before benefits began to be paid in 1942. It also retained broad support despite the exclusion of large groups of people, such as domestic workers, agricultural workers, and others groups who were disproportionately female and African American. (Legislation in later decades expanded eligibility until access was almost universal.) What became AFDC, by contrast, was controversial for decades, attacked by people who saw these benefits as an unearned "dole." It finally succumbed in 1996 to a new and more work-oriented policy of family assistance.[48]

The demise of the NRA in 1935 was mostly unlamented, even by many of those who had created it two years earlier. But there was one powerful constituency that moved immediately to restore one of its provisions: the labor movement. Workers had mobilized aggressively in 1933 and 1934 in response to Section 7(a) of the National Industrial Recovery Act, but employers had successfully resisted their demands. After the Supreme Court decision in *Schechter Poultry Corp.* v. *United States* (1935), which struck down 7(a) along with the code authorities, workers and union leaders mobilized again around an even stronger guarantee of the right of workers to bargain collectively with employers. The product of these efforts was the National Labor Relations Act of 1935, better known as the Wagner Act (after the U.S. senator from New York who had led its enactment). Roosevelt was uneasy at first about the provisions of the bill, and he signed it somewhat grudgingly. But he later changed his mind, in part because it strengthened workers' loyalty to the New Deal and the Democratic Party. The Wagner Act did more than revive Section 7(a). It also created the National Labor Relations Board (NLRB), which had the authority to police labor-management relations and use federal power to stop unfair labor practices. In 1933 business leaders had accepted Section 7(a), assuming that unions would be cooperative partners of business and government within the harmonious economy the NRA envisioned. The labor unions turned out to be adversarial organizations, however, challenging the prerogatives of business and building powers and rights of their own. The passage of the Wagner Act, in effect, marked the end of the idea of a cooperative economy and contributed to creating a more competitive one that would be increasingly characterized by the clash of powerful interest groups.[49]

Among the other legislative initiatives of 1935 were two bills designed to placate the populist anger directed at corporate power. The Public Utilities Holding Company Act sought to reduce the monopolistic power of the great utilities trusts, which Roosevelt—and many consumers—blamed for the continuing high cost of electricity. The bill, passed in August 1935, gave the government authority to break up the small number of large holding companies that dominated almost three-quarters of the market. Both opponents and supporters of the law called it the "death sentence" bill, because it appeared to threaten the survival of some great corporations. The business community fought it strenuously. But the actual results of the law were relatively modest. The Revenue Act of 1935 raised some taxes on incomes over $50,000, but the bill had little impact on government revenues and only a small impact on the wealthy. Both laws were primarily symbolic and designed, at least in part, to protect the president from public anger directed at the corporate and financial worlds.[50]

Roosevelt's response to populist rage went beyond these measures. As the 1936 election approached, the president—beginning with his January 1936 State of the Union address—developed his own harsh rhetoric directed at the "economic royalists" that so many voters had come to blame for their problems. In one of his last campaign rallies in October 1936, he unleashed an attack on what he called "the old enemies of peace...monopoly, speculation, reckless banking...[and] war profiteering," and proceeded to an extraordinary climax:

> Never before in all our history have these forces been so united against one candidate as they stand today. They are unanimous in their hate for me—and I welcome their hatred. I should like to have it said of my first Administration that in it the forces of selfishness and of lust for power met their match. I should like to have it said of my second Administration that in it these forces met their master.

Even many of Roosevelt's own allies were appalled by what one former aide called "the violence, the bombast, the naked demagoguery" of his words. But the great mass of American voters rallied to his call. Alf Landon, the Republican governor of Kansas, was Roosevelt's opponent, but Landon's campaign never dented the president's popularity. Roosevelt was reelected in 1936 by one of the greatest landslides of the twentieth century, winning 61 percent of the popular vote and carrying every state but Maine and Vermont. In Congress, Democrats now controlled 76 of the 96 seats in the Senate, and 331 out of 420 in the House.[51]

Many liberals interpreted Roosevelt's electoral victory as an endorsement of their ideas. A writer from the *Nation* said he "could see no interpretation of the returns which does not suggest that the people of America want the President to proceed along progressive or liberal lines." Others wrote of Roosevelt's "blank check," an "undreamed of success," and "no opposition worth mentioning." Few could have imagined in the glow of this great victory how quickly the Roosevelt administration would move from its remarkable triumph into a quagmire of frustration and defeat. But Roosevelt's great landslide was in some ways misleading. Many voters had supported the New Deal less because of Roosevelt's liberal agenda than because they thought he had alleviated the Depression, or because he had so effectively conveyed an image of strength and compassion. He had, like many popular leaders, attracted voters who liked him more than they liked his policies.[52]

In February 1937, emboldened by his apparent mandate, Roosevelt decided to do battle with the Supreme Court. The Court's decisions invalidating the NRA and other New Deal measures seemed to the president to threaten all his achievements and hopes. As a result, he asked Congress to enact a Court "reform" plan designed to give him the authority to appoint additional justices to the Supreme Court—one for every sitting justice over the age of 70. Roosevelt, somewhat disingenuously, claimed that the bill was designed to ease the Court's workload. But everyone understood that the real purpose was to allow the president to appoint new justices more sympathetic to the New Deal. The "Court-packing" bill, as it quickly became known, was intensely controversial and helped empower the president's conservative opposition. Congress ultimately defeated it, humiliating the president in the process. The Court itself, however, soon moved toward the center and became more amenable to New Deal programs. Legal scholars continue to argue over the reasons for the Court's shift. Was it a response to Roosevelt's threats, or was it the result of a natural evolution that had been underway for years? Whatever the reasons, the Court quickly became amenable to most of Roosevelt's achievements, especially after several conservative justices left the Court and were replaced by New Dealers.[53]

At about the same time, Roosevelt also supported an ambitious proposal to reorganize the executive branch of the federal government. The plan called for an expansion of the White House staff, the movement of the Bureau of the Budget out of the Treasury and into the White House, an increase in the president's control over the civil service and regulatory commissions, and the creation of a powerful planning mechanism within the executive branch. These proposals were the product of decades of studies and reform efforts stretching back to the beginning of the century, and they were supported by a committee of experienced municipal officials. Roosevelt's opponents, however, saw the reorganization as an attempt to consolidate still more power into the hands of the president. Congress defeated the original proposal and forced him to settle for a much more modest bill in 1939.[54]

Most damaging of all to the administration was a serious recession that began suddenly in August 1937, which seemed to be a direct result of Roosevelt's own actions. For years, goaded by his secretary of the treasury, Henry Morgenthau, Roosevelt had urged his colleagues to balance the federal budget. But the crisis of the economy had consistently thwarted such hopes. In 1937, however, Roosevelt decided that the economy was strong enough to justify cutting government spending so as to reduce the national deficit. In reality, the recovery of 1937 was fragile and incomplete, and the spending cuts contributed to a deep recession that wiped out nearly all the economic gains of the New Deal's first four years. Unemployment rapidly grew from a Depression low of 14.3 percent in 1937 to 19 percent in 1938. The gross national product, which had grown by 5.5 percent in 1937, declined by 4.5 percent in 1938. The crisis was especially traumatic to many New Dealers because it came at a point when they had begun to believe that the Depression was over. Now, confronted with the hollowness of those claims, the president joined in an agonizing reappraisal of his policies and eventually launched two important new initiatives.[55]

One was a new and energetic effort to combat "monopoly power." Opposition to monopolies had been a staple of New Deal rhetoric, although seldom of action, in 1935 and 1936. Now some of the most committed New Dealers convinced the president that the recession was a result of a deliberate effort by "economic royalists" to sabotage the economy—a "capital strike," some called it. Roosevelt responded by calling for the creation of a new commission to investigate economic conditions. The Temporary National Economic Committee, a joint investigation of Congress and the administration, spent over three years studying the effects of monopoly power, but its final report, released after World War II had begun, had no significant impact on public policy. In addition, Roosevelt's new director of the Antitrust Division of the Justice Department, Thurman Arnold, began making more energetic use of the antitrust laws than had any of his predecessors. Arnold, however, was less interested in breaking up monopolies than in imposing more regulation on them. His experiment, too, came to an end during the war.[56]

At the same time, Roosevelt was beginning to listen to liberal economists and others who argued that the recession was a result of his own spending reductions. In the spring of 1938, to the chagrin of Morgenthau, he abandoned further efforts to balance the budget. Marriner Eccles, the governor of the Federal Reserve Board, had warned the president in 1937 that Morgenthau's advice would be disastrous and had urged him to sustain spending. "A reversion to deflationary methods of balancing the budget," he wrote, "would lead to a new wave of deflation and reverse the process of recovery." The recession seemed to validate his claims, and Roosevelt, shaken by the collapse that he feared he had himself precipitated, took Eccles's advice. He secured emergency appropriations of $5 billion in spending and loans for relief and public works. It was the first time any president had explicitly endorsed the belief that stimulating mass consumption through deficit spending could promote economic growth, an idea that was rapidly gathering support among economists and public officials. The idea that federal fiscal policy was an effective tool by which government could regulate the economy, an idea associated with the British economist John Maynard Keynes, became one of the New Deal's most important policy innovations and one of its most significant legacies. Also in 1938, Roosevelt won passage of the Fair Labor Standards Act, which established a minimum wage, created a maximum forty-hour workweek, and abolished child labor, measures considered by the NRA in 1933. It, too, was part of an effort to stimulate economic growth by increasing mass purchasing power.[57]

By the end of 1938, Roosevelt was only about halfway through his presidency, but the New Deal he had created was already close to completion. In retrospect, it has sometimes seemed as significant for the things it did not do as for the things it achieved. It did not end the Great Depression and the massive unemployment that accompanied it; only the enormous public and private spending for World War II finally did that. The complaints of conservative critics notwithstanding, it did not transform American capitalism in any fundamental way. Except in the fields of labor relations and banking and finance, corporate power remained nearly as free from government regulation or control in 1945 as it had been in 1933. The New Deal did not end poverty or significantly redistribute wealth. Nor did it do very much, except symbolically, to address some of the great domestic challenges of the post-war era, among them the problems of racial and gender inequality. Despite the commitment to civil rights of Eleanor Roosevelt and such New Deal officials as Secretary of the Interior Harold Ickes, the president consistently shied away from issues that he feared would divide his party and damage his ability to work with Congress.

Even so, the domestic achievements of the Roosevelt administration rank among the most important of any presidency in American history. The New Deal created state institutions that significantly and permanently expanded the role of the federal government in American life, providing at least minimal assistance to the elderly, the poor, and the unemployed; protecting the rights of labor unions; stabilizing the banking system; building low-income housing; regulating financial markets; subsidizing agricultural production; and doing many other things that had not previously been federal responsibilities. As a result, American political and economic life became much more competitive, with workers, farmers, consumers, and others now able to press their demands upon the government in ways that in the past had usually been available only to the corporate world. Hence the frequent description of the government the New Deal created as a "broker state," a state brokering the competing claims of numerous groups. Roosevelt also produced a political coalition—the "New Deal coalition" of farmers, workers, the poor and unemployed, African Americans in northern cities, traditional progressives, and committed new liberals—that made the Democratic Party the majority party in national politics, a position it retained for more than a generation after the New Deal's own end. Finally, the Roosevelt administration generated a set of political ideas, known to later generations as New Deal liberalism, that remained a source of inspiration and controversy for decades and that helped shape the next major experiments in liberal reform, the New Frontier and the Great Society of the 1960s.

That the New Deal sputtered to something like a close in Roosevelt's second term was partly because the political tides were turning against him. In 1938, and again in 1942, Democrats suffered considerable losses in congressional elections, and the emerging conservative coalition of Republicans and southern Democrats was now capable of blocking almost anything the White House proposed. But the New Deal faded as well because of the president's growing preoccupation with the greatest catastrophe of the twentieth century, the spiraling global crisis that led Europe, Asia, and ultimately the United States into World War II.[58]

The global conflict that became the Second World War began even before Roosevelt entered office. Japan's military leaders gained control of their country's government and launched an invasion of Manchuria in 1931, over the strenuous objections of China and the United States. Mussolini seized power in Italy in 1922 and soon began arming his country for war. And Adolf Hitler established himself as the most powerful political figure in Germany in 1932, became Chancellor in 1933, and quickly began to expand German military power.

Roosevelt was aware of these events, of course, but he was slow to engage with the world, as his repudiation of the London Economic Conference seemed to suggest. He abandoned Hoover's efforts to settle the issue of World War I debts through international agreements and, instead, forbade American banks to make loans to institutions (mostly in Europe) that had failed to repay their loans to the United States. He took these seemingly isolationist actions not because he was uninterested in global issues. Indeed, he recognized earlier than most people the dangers that the growth of dictatorships and rearmament posed. But in the desperate economic circumstances he faced in his first years in office, he focused mostly on domestic issues and made only faint gestures toward the need for stability in the larger world.[59]

He did, however, take a strong position on international trade from the beginning of his presidency. He supported a significant tariff reduction (in effect repealing the 1930 Smoot-Hawley Tariff, which most economists even at the time agreed had contributed to the contraction of the economy). The Reciprocal Trade Agreement Act of 1934 reduced many tariffs by half and helped pressure other nations to do the same. The desire to increase international trade also drove Roosevelt's efforts to improve relations with the Soviet Union, a nation that most American leaders had viewed with suspicion and mistrust since the Bolshevik Revolution of 1917. In November 1933 he met in Washington with the Russian foreign minister, Maxim Litvinov, and agreed to establish diplomatic relations with the Soviet regime. In return, Litvinov promised to cease propaganda efforts in the United States and to protect American citizens in Russia. The new relationship did not, however, produce any significant increase in trade.[60]

Roosevelt's most important international initiative during his first years in office was what came to be known as the "Good Neighbor Policy," an effort to improve diplomatic and economic relations with Latin America. To advance this goal, Roosevelt repudiated the use of military force in policing economic agreements in Latin America and announced that "no state has the right to intervene in the internal or external affairs of another." The new policy helped more than double trade between the United States and Latin America in the 1930s, and it also lowered the temperature of American relations with its neighbors. U.S. economic dominance in many areas of Latin America continued, and even expanded, in the 1930s and 1940s, but with a significantly reduced level of conflict and animus.[61]

Roosevelt's preoccupation with international trade and finance in his first two years in office could not long survive the growing militarism of Italy, Germany, and Japan—and the threat of war this militarism posed to the world. Roosevelt was, at heart, a Wilsonian internationalist (as was his secretary of state, Cordell Hull), but he was also a veteran of the political failure of Wilson's great vision. He was determined to expand the role of the United States in the world, but he also remained cautious about the pace of change. In January 1935 Roosevelt asked the Senate to approve a treaty that would allow the United States to join the World Court, a judicial body created by the League of Nations in 1920 and designed to mediate international disputes. Domestic opposition to the treaty was strong. The Hearst papers launched a fierce campaign against the court, and Father Coughlin reached out to his vast radio audience to urge his listeners to protest what he considered a surrender of national autonomy to "the international bankers." Enough members of Congress were intimidated by the anti-treaty campaign to prevent ratification. The defeat was a stinging blow to Roosevelt, who was slow to make such an effort again.[62]

But the world did not cooperate with Roosevelt's reticence. In the fall of 1935, Mussolini's army invaded Ethiopia. The United States declined to cooperate with a League of Nations oil boycott of Italy to protest the Italian aggression. In July 1936 Francisco Franco began a military insurrection against the elected government of Spain, with support from Nazi Germany. Civil war ravaged the nation for almost three years. None of the great powers chose to challenge Franco's insurrection, although several hundred American volunteers created the Abraham Lincoln Brigade and joined the Republican opposition, without any support from the U.S. government. Franco finally consolidated control of Spain in 1939.[63]

In July 1937 Japan—which had seized large parts of Manchuria several years earlier—launched a full-scale war against China and quickly captured Shanghai, the commercial capital of the nation, and Nanking, its political capital. The fate of China was of more concern to many Americans than were the fates of Ethiopia and Spain. There was, nevertheless, strong public opposition to taking action against the Japanese, even after they attacked and sunk an American gunboat, the *Panay*. The Japanese government apologized for the incident, and most of the American public, eager to avoid conflict, decided to overlook the attack. There was little support for any significant American effort to stop Japanese aggression. In October 1937 the president made a tentative effort to change public opinion. He delivered a speech in Chicago (the home of the rabidly isolationist and anti-Roosevelt *Chicago Tribune*), in which he warned of "the epidemic of world lawlessness" and proposed a relatively modest challenge. "When an epidemic of physical disease starts to spread," Roosevelt argued, "the community approves and joins in a quarantine of patients in order to protect the health of community against the spread of disease." War, he argued, was also a kind of "contagion," and it required a similar quarantine against aggression. "There is no escape through mere isolation or neutrality," he concluded. But what became known as the "Quarantine Speech" not only failed to change public opinion, but also inflamed isolationist sentiment. Roosevelt, shaken by the ferocity of the criticism he received, took no steps to implement a policy that would make a "quarantine" meaningful. In 1938, when British prime minister Neville Chamberlain met with Hitler at Munich and ceded Czechoslovakia to the Nazis in exchange for what turned out to be a hollow promise of peace, Roosevelt cabled Chamberlain with congratulations.[64]

When war finally broke out in Europe in September 1939, Roosevelt continued to insist that the conflict would not involve the United States. But he also took pains to differentiate his policies from those Woodrow Wilson announced in 1914. Wilson had insisted that the United States would be neutral in "thought, word, and deed." Roosevelt declared, "This nation will remain a neutral nation, but I cannot ask that every American remain neutral in thought as well." Despite the political risks, his support for Britain and its allies was clear and unequivocal from the start.

In the spring of 1940, the war spread quickly throughout western Europe. The German "blitzkrieg" through the Low Countries and into northern France drove the defeated British and French armies from the Continent. Virtually all of Europe was now under Nazi domination. In response to these calamitous events, American public opinion began to move slowly toward more active American support for Britain. Roosevelt moved with this shift in sentiment and at times stepped somewhat ahead of it. First, he managed to persuade Congress to repeal the Neutrality Acts it had passed in the 1930s, thus making it possible for the United States to begin selling weapons and other supplies to Britain on a "cash and carry" basis. In September 1940, in response to England's financial problems and significant pressure from influential internationalists, Roosevelt traded fifty American destroyers to the British in exchange for several British bases in the Caribbean. The "destroyers-for-bases deal" was in some ways a subterfuge for helping to reinforce the British navy, but it also gave the United States a valuable new foothold in the Caribbean.[65]

In part, Roosevelt's caution in supporting Britain was a result of the impending presidential election and his concern about moving beyond public opinion so soon before the vote. Although several had tried, no president had ever served more than two terms in the White House. Roosevelt was cautious about breaking this longstanding precedent. He declined to announce his candidacy for reelection, and he spoke often of his desire to return to his home in Hyde Park (where he was already planning what became the first presidential library). At times he showed support for various potential successors. But he was careful never to allow any one candidate to gain wide support. As a result, by the time of the convention there was—as Roosevelt had planned—no one capable of challenging his renomination.[66]

In the meantime, Republicans began rallying around an unorthodox candidate: Wendell Willkie, a former Democrat who had attracted the attention of internationalists within the party. They helped persuade him to run. He was an attractive, energetic, charismatic figure. Despite a long career as a prominent industrialist who lived on Fifth Avenue in New York, he emphasized his roots in small-town Indiana and repudiated many of the most conservative positions of his party. At the June Republican convention in Philadelphia—with strong support from such Republican press barons as Henry Luce of *Time* and *Life* magazines and Roy Howard of the Scripps-Howard newspaper chain, and from a grass-roots movement organized by a resourceful young lawyer—Willkie was nominated on the sixth ballot. A month later, the Democrats assembled in Chicago (the site of Roosevelt's memorable 1932 nomination) still without any public indication of the president's intentions. By then, Roosevelt was intent on winning renomination, but he remained determined not to be viewed as seeking an unprecedented third term. His supporters, therefore, made unusual efforts to create the image of a true draft. As balloting was about to begin, a voice from a loudspeaker began booming through the hall: "We want Roosevelt," a chant that the carefully chosen audience in the galleries immediately echoed. Roosevelt was nominated on the first ballot. Over the objections of his more conservative advisors, he chose as his running mate Secretary of Agriculture Henry Wallace, one of the staunch progressives who had joined the New Deal in 1933.[67]

Willkie's nomination was designed in part to attract moderate Democratic voters. But Roosevelt had already moved to attract moderate Republicans to his own candidacy. In June, he appointed two prominent Republicans to important Cabinet posts, something Woodrow Wilson, at great cost, had famously refused to do during and after World War I. Henry Stimson—secretary of war under Taft and secretary of state under Hoover—once again became the head of the War Department. Frank Knox, a newspaper editor and 1936 Republican candidate for vice president, agreed to become secretary of the navy. As a result, the differences between the two candidates on international issues seemed relatively modest. Willkie and Roosevelt quietly agreed not to make the war an issue in the campaign, although that proved a difficult agreement to keep. Both men supported the controversial creation of a draft in September 1940. But the election continued to be dominated by the question of whether or not the

United States would enter the war. Willkie argued that Roosevelt was much more likely to send American soldiers into war than he would be. Roosevelt responded a few days before the election with his own disingenuous assurance during a speech in Boston, in which he said: "I have said this before, but I shall say it again and again: Your boys are not going to be sent into any foreign wars." He even dropped his earlier qualification: "except in case of attack." The campaign was closer than his first two elections, but Roosevelt won decisively nevertheless, with 55 percent of the popular vote and a 449–82 electoral majority.[68]

With the election behind him, and with public opinion moving heavily in favor of American aid to Britain, Roosevelt intensified his own attempts to support the British war effort. The London Treasury announced that it had no foreign exchange with which to pay for American goods; Winston Churchill, who had been elected prime minister in May 1940, wrote Roosevelt that Britain faced "mortal danger" if the United States did not help sustain the imperiled Royal Navy. Roosevelt proposed a new program of aid to Britain that he called "Lend-Lease," a system designed to permit the British to continue receiving armaments from the United States without paying cash for them. He compared it to lending a neighbor a garden hose "to help put out his fire." But what the Lend-Lease Act actually did was use $7 billion in congressional appropriations to provide Britain with war supplies. Despite fierce resistance from isolationists in and out of office, Congress approved the program in March 1941. The United States, Roosevelt said, must become "the great arsenal of democracy."[69]

Gradually, American assistance to the Allies grew even more overt. As German submarines imperiled the convoys that were shipping American goods across the Atlantic, American naval vessels began patrolling the ocean and escorting convoys of merchant ships heading for Britain. U.S. law forbade the American navy from attacking German ships or submarines, but Roosevelt quietly and slowly (too slowly, according to some members of his administration) began to authorize more direct attacks—especially after German submarines attacked the U.S. destroyer *Greer* in early September. Roosevelt seized on that incident to announce that "American naval vessels and American planes will no longer wait until Axis submarines...strike their deadly blow." By late September, the United States was, in effect, in an undeclared naval war with Germany.[70]

Additional evidence of Roosevelt's commitment to war was his August 1941 meeting with Churchill aboard an American cruiser off Newfoundland. They signed what later became known as the Atlantic Charter, a statement of war aims that included "the right of all peoples to choose the form of government under which they will live...the final destruction of the Nazi tyranny...[and] a peace which will afford to all nations the means of dwelling in safety...[so that] all the men in all the lands may live out their lives in freedom from fear and want." In November 1941, shortly after Hitler invaded Russia, Roosevelt extended lend-lease assistance to the Soviet Union, the first step toward forging an important new wartime alliance.[71]

At the same time that the conflict with Germany was intensifying in the Atlantic, the United States was increasing its opposition to Japanese aggression in China. Washington imposed a trade embargo on Japan and froze Japanese assets in the United States. Roosevelt justified this step as a way to pressure the Japanese to abandon the war, but he had no realistic hope that this would be the result. Without access to American petroleum, the Japanese had little choice but to seek new sources of oil. Roosevelt and his aides assumed that Japan's next step would be to seize the oil-producing British and Dutch possessions in the Pacific. Instead, on December 7, 1941, a wave of Japanese bombers struck the American naval base in Pearl Harbor, Hawaii, killing more than 2,000 American servicemen and damaging or destroying dozens of ships and airplanes. American intelligence had earlier broken the Japanese codes and knew an attack on the territory of one of the Western powers was coming. The information Washington received, if properly interpreted, could have alerted the United States to Tokyo's target. But because no one anticipated that the Japanese would launch so bold an effort, no one predicted what they actually did. The surprise attack on Hawaii was an extraordinary military achievement, but it did not achieve its goal of crippling the American Pacific fleet. By a fortunate accident, no American aircraft carriers were in the harbor that day, and many of the damaged ships in Pearl Harbor were soon repaired. The attack did, however, galvanize the American public and created overwhelming support for war. "So we have won after all," Winston Churchill noted when he heard the news. With the United States in the war, he believed, the victory of the Allies was now assured.[72]

The next day Roosevelt traveled to Capitol Hill to ask Congress for a declaration of war. "Yesterday, December 7, 1941—a date which will live in infamy," he grimly announced, "the United States of America was suddenly and deliberately attacked by the naval and air forces of the Empire of Japan." Within hours, the Senate and the House voted for a declaration of war—the Senate unanimously, and the House by a vote of 388 to 1 (the lone dissenter being a pacifist congresswoman who had also voted against entry into World War I). Three days later, Germany and Italy, Japan's European allies, declared war on the United States, and the American Congress quickly and unanimously reciprocated. The United States was now fully engaged in the largest war in history.[73]

Roosevelt's life during the war years was both more con-
stricted and more independent than it had been during
his first two terms as president. The combination of his
own paralysis and intensified wartime security meant
that the president traveled less often and spent most
of his time in the White House, by then a somewhat
decrepit and uncomfortable building, swelteringly hot
in the summer (despite the recent installation of air con-
ditioning in a few rooms) and poorly ventilated in the
winter. The imperious presidential housekeeper, Henri-
etta Nesbit, oversaw meals so bland and poorly prepared
that Roosevelt's dinner companions often ate elsewhere
before joining him. It was in many ways a lonely life.
Not long after Pearl Harbor, Franklin proposed that
Eleanor resume her role as a true partner to him, that

they restore, in effect, their long-fractured marriage. But Eleanor declined and continued to spend much of her time away from Washington, touring military bases and spending long periods in the home she built for herself in Dutchess County, on the grounds of the Roosevelt estate in Hyde Park. For decades, Roosevelt's closest companion had been Missy LeHand, but in 1941 she suffered a severe stroke that left her incapacitated for the last three years of his life. Whatever private grief Roosevelt might have felt at the end of his relationship with LeHand was not visible to those around him. He never visited her during her illness, even during the many months she remained in the White House. Instead, he surrounded himself with other adoring women: his flamboyant cousin, Polly Delano; the young and attractive Queen Marguerite of Norway, who took refuge in Washington during the war and spent much time in the White House; and Margaret "Daisy" Suckley, an unmarried, middle-aged distant cousin who began accompanying Roosevelt in the mid-1930s and became his constant companion (inconspicuous to others but essential to him) throughout the war years.[74]

The high level of security may have cut Roosevelt off from many things, but the heightened protection also gave him an increased sphere of personal privacy. In 1941 he again began seeing Lucy Mercer (now Lucy Mercer Rutherford, whose wealthy husband had recently been incapacitated by a stroke). Their occasional meetings, carefully hidden, took place mostly outside the White House, during automobile trips into the countryside or through Washington's Rock Creek Park. They were a reminder of his youth and his lost romantic life.[75]

Roosevelt's other frequent companions were the members of his own White House staff: military aides, political and policy advisers, and others. His most important colleague for a time was Harry Hopkins, no longer "minister of relief" but Roosevelt's most trusted envoy to America's wartime allies, especially Churchill and Stalin. For a substantial period during the war, Hopkins lived in the White House, fighting the war at the same time that he was fighting the stomach cancer that led to his death in 1945.[76]

Throughout the war, Roosevelt also maintained an intense relationship with Winston Churchill, with whom he carried on a voluminous correspondence. Roosevelt assigned some of his own aides to serve as liaisons to London, and Churchill sent some of his colleagues to work in the White House. Churchill himself came to Washington repeatedly, spending weeks at a time in the White House planning strategy and sharing cocktails and meals. Their relationship was not always easy, however. Churchill was Roosevelt's constant goad, requesting more aid and a more aggressive military posture. He was also a heavy drinker who liked to stay up late into the night, which disrupted Roosevelt's quieter routine. In their meetings, Roosevelt was his usual evasive and politically cautious self, to Churchill's frequent dismay. Nevertheless, their partnership was one of the most important of the twentieth century. "It is fun to be in the same decade with you," Roosevelt cabled Churchill in 1941. Churchill later wrote, "I felt I was in contact with a very great man who was also a warm-hearted friend and the foremost champion of the high causes which we served."[77]

Roosevelt was somewhat more detached from everyday decision-making as a war leader than he had been as a domestic one. He relied heavily on Henry Stimson and the talented young War Department staff, as well as on his own military aides, for the day-to-day management of the war. But he participated decisively in major strategic decisions. Almost immediately after Pearl Harbor, Roosevelt made what was perhaps the most important of those decisions. There was considerable public and elite sentiment for giving first priority to the defeat of Japan, both because it had been the Japanese who had first attacked the United States and because of the large and powerful group of Americans with strong ties to China. Roosevelt, however, decided otherwise. He committed the United States to a two-front war, and he devoted considerable resources to the Pacific front. But he insisted that the United States give first priority to the conflict in Europe. Even after making that first and critical decision, disagreements continued. Roosevelt wanted to devote virtually all the Allied resources to preparing an invasion across the English Channel into France, the most direct route to Germany. Churchill and other British leaders, remembering the terrible carnage in France during World War I, preferred to delay the major invasion and begin with smaller incursions along the periphery of the Nazi empire. Roosevelt finally sided with Churchill, partly because he realized that it would take a long time to build enough capacity to allow a cross-channel invasion, and partly because he was reluctant to keep American forces inactive for so long. He supported the British proposal to begin engaging the Germans in the territories they had seized in North Africa. An Allied invasion of North Africa began in November 1942, with simultaneous Anglo-American assaults on Casablanca, Oran, and Algiers. The Allies captured all three ports within days, and by early spring they had driven the German forces out of most of North Africa. The Allied forces then continued across the Mediterranean, invading Sicily and southern Italy in the summer of 1943.

Although American forces in the Pacific received less than a fifth of the total resources the nation devoted to the war in these early years, they pursued an active strategy against the Japanese. Having been driven from virtually the entire Pacific Ocean west of Hawaii, and having lost the Philippines within a few months of Pearl Harbor, American forces began striking back and soon won two critical victories, first in the battle of the Coral Sea in May 1942, and then in the battle of Midway a month later. From there the United States launched a series of offensives against Japanese outposts in the Solomon Islands, just north of Australia, in the first of several prolonged and savage island campaigns that continued for the duration of the war.

Throughout 1942 and 1943, while the battles in North Africa and the Pacific continued, Roosevelt remained preoccupied with the ongoing debate over how and when to launch an Allied invasion of France. The Soviet Union was now bearing the brunt of the German war effort, and Soviet leader Joseph Stalin argued that Anglo-American forces must move quickly to open another front in Europe in order to prevent the collapse of the Russian offensive against Germany. Roosevelt and Churchill met in Casablanca, Morocco, in January 1943, where they agreed to try to mollify Stalin by declaring their support for nothing less than "unconditional surrender" of the Axis powers. In other words, the United States and Britain would not leave the Soviet Union to fight alone by agreeing to a separate peace.

In November 1943 Roosevelt and Churchill traveled to Tehran for their first face-to-face meeting with Stalin. By then, the war in eastern Europe had turned decisively in favor of the Soviet Union, which meant that Roosevelt and Churchill now had little leverage over Stalin. Even so, Stalin agreed to enter the Pacific war after the fighting in Europe came to an end. Roosevelt and Churchill promised to launch the long-delayed invasion of France in the spring of 1944. The meeting produced less agreement on other matters. The Western leaders mostly avoided taking a stand on Stalin's plans to keep the areas of Poland that the Soviet Union had seized in 1939.

In the meantime, Roosevelt turned his attention increasingly to the shape of the postwar world. He persuaded twenty-six nations to sign the United Nations Declaration, a statement of principles based on the Atlantic Charter that would—after his death—lead to the creation of the United Nations. In July 1944 he convened an international conference at Bretton Woods, New Hampshire, that created the International Monetary Fund, charged with stabilizing global currencies, and the International Bank for Reconstruction and Development, established to assist the shattered nations of Europe and Asia in rebuilding after the war.

C

At home, massive wartime spending ended the Depression and launched a period of vigorous economic growth. But it also created extraordinary challenges for the government in managing the unprecedented industrial production that the war required. During World War I, Woodrow Wilson had created the War Industries Board, which had substantial power to control the distribution of materials and to force industries to comply with the government's needs. Its director, Bernard Baruch, wielded extraordinary power. In 1941 there were demands for a similarly powerful agency. But Roosevelt was reluctant to create so great a center of authority. In 1939 he created the War Resources Board to plan the mobilization for war, but it was a weak agency that soon collapsed under its own bureaucratic weight. The president replaced it with the Office of Emergency Management, which would work with the National Defense Advisory Commission. This cumbersome system lasted only six months before it was replaced by the new Office of Production Management (OPM), which also failed to solve the production chaos. In the summer of 1941, Roosevelt created yet another new agency, the Supply Priorities and Allocation Board, to operate in tandem with OPM. To those who continued to admire the model of Baruch in World War I, and there were many such admirers in Washington, these early war agencies had one great, glaring deficiency: the absence of a strong leader capable of bringing order to the industrial conversion to war. But creating a new Baruch (or restoring Baruch himself to his former prominence) was precisely what Roosevelt was trying to avoid.

In January 1942, in an effort to stave off the growing criticism of the production bureaucracies, Roosevelt announced yet another agency, the War Production Board (WPB). Its director was Donald Nelson, a former Sears Roebuck executive who had been working in earlier production agencies for two years. For a while, the new board generated broad enthusiasm. Nelson had "authority greater than any U.S. citizen except the President himself has ever had," *Time* exclaimed, "greater even than that wielded by...Baruch" during World War I. "It is the biggest single job in the world today," *Life* claimed. But Nelson was no

Baruch. Indeed, Roosevelt may have been attracted to him precisely because he seemed so unlikely to be an "economic czar." Nelson was, in reality, an ingratiating and palpably unambitious man who would not be likely to challenge the president's own preeminence. Over time, the WPB came to seem almost as ineffectual as its many predecessors. Within a year, Roosevelt was again creating new agencies that competed with, and undermined, the WPB. In 1944 he established the Office of War Mobilization (OWM), directed by James F. Byrnes, a former U.S. senator from South Carolina and associate justice of the Supreme Court. The OWM was lodged in the White House, which is where Roosevelt had wanted it almost from the start.[78]

The problem with the war agencies was not primarily that they impeded production. American industry was producing an unprecedented amount of armaments and supplies, including airplanes, ships, tanks, jeeps, ammunition, uniforms, rubber, oil, and other products essential to the war effort. Civilians became accustomed to shortages of goods that were important to the war effort. The Office of Price Administration rationed tires, gasoline, butter, and other goods reasonably efficiently. In the meantime, millions of newly employed workers began to earn significant wages again and, given the absence of consumer products, saved much of their income, which helped sustain economic growth after the war ended.[79]

From the first days of the war mobilization to the last, the principal complaint about the process was not inadequate production. It was that the government was turning over too much authority (and too many profits) to industrialists. Particular criticism was directed at the "dollar-a-year men," executives—mostly from large firms—who had official appointments in the war bureaucracy but who continued to receive their corporate salaries. They dominated the war agencies and, not surprisingly, tended to favor their own companies and those like them. The government had few alternatives, however. Just as the NRA had lacked the expertise and experience to manage the industrial economy in the early 1930s, the wartime agencies lacked the knowledge and skill to oversee wartime production. Without the "dollar-a-year men," the machinery of mobilization would likely have been much less effective. Other critics were concerned about what they considered "discrimination" against small businesses in the awarding of contracts. Indeed, most small businesses did find themselves largely shut out of war production, and Congress created the Smaller War Plants Corporation in 1942 to ensure that not all contracts went to large producers. Roosevelt supported the effort but never gave the agency enough authority to challenge existing patterns effectively.[80]

Roosevelt promoted no significant domestic reform legislation during the war, and after the 1942 elections,

which increased the power of congressional conservatives, he was unable to prevent the dismantling of many
New Deal agencies, among them the WPA. But what he
could not do legislatively, he tried to do rhetorically. Even
before Pearl Harbor, he described an ambitious vision of a
peacetime society in which the government would ensure
a minimal level of comfort and security for all Americans.
He labeled it the Four Freedoms: "freedom of speech,
freedom of religion, freedom from want, and freedom
from fear." Three years later, he proposed "a second Bill
of Rights...an economic bill of rights," which would
guarantee every citizen a living wage, decent housing,
health care, and education, as well as additional support
for the elderly, disabled, and unemployed. Little came at
the time of these broad promises of universal security, but
Roosevelt secured a portion of these programs through the
Servicemen's Readjustment Act of 1944, better known as
the "G.I. Bill of Rights," which provided generous housing, educational, medical, and other benefits to veterans
when the war ended.[81]

ε

Roosevelt was less receptive to the demands of the many Americans who sought to harness the war effort to greater moral causes. In 1940, largely because of heavy pressure by African-American leaders, he created the Fair Employment Practices Commission to enhance black employment opportunities in war industries. This was the first federal agency since Reconstruction to be actively engaged in the effort to promote racial equality. Roosevelt did not, however, respond to many other demands for racial equality, despite his personal opposition to segregation and his wife's very public support for racial equality. The armed forces remained segregated throughout the war, and while African-American leaders promoted the idea of the "Double-V"—a simultaneous commitment to victory in the war and victory over racism at home—there was little progress toward such goals before 1945.[82]

In 1942, shortly after the attack on Pearl Harbor, the president approved a proposal from military officials on the West Coast to "intern" the thousands of resident Japanese Americans living in California. There was no evidence to suggest that they were in any way disloyal. Many of them had been born in the United States, and others were naturalized citizens. Attorney General Francis Biddle strongly opposed the relocation of the Japanese Americans, but Roosevelt deferred to the War Department, which supported the plan. Thousands of families were transferred from their homes to internment camps located mostly in the deserts, and many of them were not released until 1944. It was one of the greatest violations of civil liberties in American history.[83]

To many Americans, at the time and since, the greatest moral failure of the United States in the war years was its seeming unwillingness to take forceful action to save the Jews in Europe, who, beginning in 1941, were being systematically exterminated by Nazi Germany. Six million Jews, and two million others, died in this unparalleled act of genocide. In fairness, there was little the United States could have done to save most of those imperiled by the Holocaust after 1939, other than win the war. But the United States gave little help to Jews attempting to escape from Europe before the war began, and it offered refuge to very few of those imperiled people on the edges of the Nazi empire who might have been rescuable. Early in 1944, Roosevelt—increasingly alarmed by reports of the Holocaust that had been flowing into America since 1942—created the War Refugee Board, which provided authority and funds to help refugees escape from Europe. In the end, however, it managed to remove fewer than a thousand Jews from danger. In a gesture that had little impact on the war, but had a significant impact on its aftermath, Roosevelt, with the support of Churchill and Stalin, promised to create tribunals to try "war criminals" after the war—a step that led to the postwar trials in Nuremberg and Tokyo.[84]

In July 1944 Roosevelt, having left his intentions vague for months, announced his candidacy for a fourth term. "All that is within me cries out to go back to my home on the Hudson River," he claimed, "but the future existence of the nation and the future existence of our chosen form of government are at stake." He had, he said, "as little right to withdraw as the soldier has to leave his post in the line." At the convention, Roosevelt acquiesced to the demand of party leaders that he abandon his controversial vice president, Henry Wallace, whose increasingly left-leaning views alarmed many in the party. The president himself was fearful of splitting the party and alienating conservatives. He chose instead Harry S. Truman, a moderate senator from Missouri who had attracted favorable publicity for his effective chairmanship of the wartime Senate Committee to Investigate the National Defense Program. Roosevelt did not appear at the convention himself, but was instead renominated by the Chicago convention while he was reviewing a naval exercise in San Diego.[85]

By then, Roosevelt was in increasingly dire health, a result of decades of smoking and the cumulative impact of years of physical inaction. He refused to acknowledge his deteriorating condition, which his doctors diagnosed as advanced arteriosclerosis, and which forced him to live much of the time as a virtual invalid. His once robust body now looked withered. His face was pale and gaunt. He often could not hold a teacup steady enough to keep it from spilling. He was frequently fatigued and sometimes completely incapacitated by attacks of angina. He remained as preoccupied with the war as his deteriorating condition allowed, but he took only slight interest in the presidential campaign.

After the convention, Roosevelt did virtually no campaigning until rumors of his declining health became a factor in the election. At that point he rallied for several effective appearances, including some vigorous speeches in October and a brutal motorcade through New York City in pouring rain, which seemed to prove that he was fit to serve another term. He defeated the Republican candidate, Governor Thomas E. Dewey of New York—a man he had come to despise—with 53 percent of the vote and a much larger electoral majority. Roosevelt cancelled the traditional Inauguration at the Capitol and was sworn in from the south portico of the White House, after which he delivered an inaugural address of less than ten minutes in length, the shortest in history.[86]

One of the many reasons for Roosevelt's political resilience was that the Allied war effort was by then clearly on the road to victory. On June 6, 1944, Allied forces landed on the Normandy coast and began a successful invasion of France. By August they had liberated Paris, and by mid-September they had driven the Germans almost entirely out of France. The invasion bogged down for a time later that fall, but in the early spring of 1945, the Anglo-American advance on Germany resumed. At the same time, Soviet forces swept westward into central Europe and the Balkans. By the spring of 1945, American forces in the Pacific had captured almost all the strategic islands east of Japan, retaken the Philippines, and closed in on Japan itself.

Unknown to all but a few, the United States was by then far along in an effort Roosevelt had authorized early in the war: the Manhattan Project, a vast scientific undertaking to design and build an atomic bomb. The project was spurred by fears that Germany was working on a similar weapon at the same time. In July 1945, three months after Roosevelt's death, the first atomic bomb was detonated in a desert in New Mexico. There is little evidence to suggest how Roosevelt might have used the new weapon had he lived. (His successor, Harry Truman, authorized the use of atomic bombs against two Japanese cities—Hiroshima and Nagasaki—after Roosevelt's death.)[87]

In January 1945, with victory in Europe apparently imminent, Roosevelt traveled secretly to Yalta on the Crimean coast for another meeting with Churchill and Stalin. Both men were shocked at the president's wasted physical appearance. But Roosevelt participated actively and capably in the negotiations. The three leaders agreed on the postwar occupation of Germany, which would be temporarily divided among the occupying powers. Stalin agreed to join the Pacific war once the conflict in Europe was over. They all agreed to the creation of what was to become the United Nations, but they could reach no accord on the future of Poland. Stalin had already created a new Polish government dominated by people loyal to the Soviet Union; the exiled prewar Polish government, now in London, was also intent on establishing its own authority over the nation. Stalin's forces were already poised to occupy Poland, and there was little that Roosevelt and Churchill could do to stop him. Faced with an impasse, the three leaders papered over their differences with a series of weak and unenforceable compromises. Roosevelt returned home still hoping that he could eventually reach some agreement with Stalin. While he did not realize it at the time, the outlines of the coming Cold War were already visible at Yalta.[88]

Early in April, Roosevelt left Washington for a vacation at his retreat in Warm Springs, Georgia, accompanied by his cousins and several aides. On April 12, he received a visit from Lucy Rutherford, who brought an artist with her to paint a portrait of the president. Roosevelt posed while seated at a small table in his cabin, where he was working on a Jefferson Day speech. Suddenly he looked up and complained of a "terrific headache." Moments later he collapsed from a massive stroke, from which he never regained consciousness. He died several hours later.[89]

In the decades since his death, Franklin Roosevelt's stature as the most important leader of the twentieth century has not diminished. Even those critical of his achievements recognize their magnitude: the reshaping of American government, the transformation of the Democratic Party, the redefinition of American liberalism, the successful leadership of the United States through the greatest war in world history, and the reconstruction of America's relationship to the international order. Such achievements were not his alone, but it is only necessary to look at the world that Roosevelt inherited in 1932 and what it had become by the time of his death to understand the importance of his leadership in these critical years. They were years during which a prostrate nation slowly rose to its feet. They were years during which democracy struggled with powerful alternatives—fascism and communism—and during which Roosevelt vied with Adolf Hitler and Josef Stalin for the future of nations. And they were years that pitted Churchill's defense of imperialism against Roosevelt's commitment to self-determination for all people. The postwar world was not a perfect one, of course, and Roosevelt was not a perfect leader. His confidence that Stalin would cooperate in building a stable and consensual world order was probably doomed from the start. The atomic weapons he set in motion, but did not live to see, escalated the danger of warfare and continue to imperil the world. Serious injustices in American society remained unaddressed. But the years since World War II—for the United States and for much of the world—have reflected the values Roosevelt defended far more successfully than they have those of his rivals. His efforts helped preserve democracy for hundreds of millions of people across the world and gave hope to millions more. No president since Lincoln has faced such daunting crises and challenges, and none has surmounted them with such boldness and confidence. It is little wonder that he remains, in the minds of most Americans, a figure who sits alongside Washington and Lincoln as part of the triumvirate of our greatest leaders. "History will honor this man for many things, however wide the disagreement of many of his countrymen with some of his policies and actions," the *New York Times* wrote the day after Roosevelt's death, already defining his legacy. "It will honor him above all else because he had the vision to see clearly the supreme crisis of our times and the courage to meet that crisis boldly. Men will thank God on their knees, a hundred years from now, that Franklin D. Roosevelt was in the White House."[90]

Notes

1. Frank Freidel, *Franklin D. Roosevelt: The Apprenticeship* (Boston: Little, Brown, 1952), 3–34.

2. Geoffrey C. Ward, *Before the Trumpet: Young Franklin Roosevelt, 1882–1905* (New York: Harper & Row, 1985), 109–177.

3. Ward, *Before the Trumpet*, 178–209; Freidel, *The Apprenticeship*, 35–51.

4. Jean Edward Smith, *FDR* (New York: Random House, 2007), 29–33; Freidel, *The Apprenticeship*, 57; Geoffrey C. Ward, *A First-Class Temperament: The Emergence of Franklin Roosevelt* (New York: Harper & Row, 1989), 46–47.

5. Jonathan Alter, *The Defining Moment: FDR's Hundred Days and the Triumph of Hope* (New York: Simon & Schuster, 2006), 28–35.

6. Blanche Wiesen Cook, *Eleanor Roosevelt*, vol. 1, *1884–1933* (New York: Viking, 1992), 125–162; Joseph P. Lash,

Eleanor and Franklin (New York: W. W. Norton, 1971), 101–141.

7. Freidel, *The Apprenticeship*, 97–156.

8. Ward, *A First-Class Temperament*, 199–262, 439–443.

9. Cook, *Eleanor Roosevelt*, 1:229–236; Lash, *Eleanor and Franklin*, 220–227.

10. Frank Freidel, *Franklin Roosevelt: The Ordeal* (New York: Little, Brown, 1954), 51–69.

11. John Milton Cooper Jr., *The Warrior and the Priest: Woodrow Wilson and Theodore Roosevelt* (Cambridge, MA: Harvard University Press, 1983); Thomas J. Knock, *To End All Wars: Woodrow Wilson and the Quest for a New World Order* (New York: Oxford University Press, 1992); Michael McGerr, *A Fierce Discontent: The Rise and Fall of the Progressive Movement in America, 1870–1920* (New York: The Free Press, 2003); Richard Hofstadter, *The American Political Tradition and the Men Who Made It* (New York: Alfred A. Knopf, 1948), 206–282.

12. Freidel, *The Ordeal*, 92–98.

13. Ward, *A First-Class Temperament*, 576–626; Freidel, *The Ordeal*, 92–105.

14. Ward, *A First-Class Temperament*, 601–641.

15. Freidel, *The Ordeal*, 92–105; Ward, *A First-Class Temperament*, chapters 16–17; Hugh Gregory Gallagher, *FDR's Splendid Deception* (New York: Dodd, Mead, 1985), 89–105.

16. David Burner, *The Politics of Provincialism: The Democratic Party in Transition, 1918–1932* (New York: W. W. Norton, 1967), 75–102.

17. Freidel, *The Ordeal,* 160–183; Burner, *The Politics of Provincialism*, 114–125.

18. Elliott Roosevelt, ed., *F.D.R.: His Personal Letters, 1928–1945* (New York: Duell, Sloan, and Pearce, 1950), 184–185.

19. Arthur M. Schlesinger Jr., *The Age of Roosevelt: The Crisis of the Old Order, 1919–1933* (Boston: Houghton Mifflin Company, 1957), 413–420.

20. Schlesinger, *Crisis of the Old Order*, 420–439; Samuel I. Rosenman, ed., *The Public Papers and Addresses of Franklin D. Roosevelt* (New York: Russell and Russell, 1938–1950), I: 742–756.

21. Rexford G. Tugwell, *In Search of Roosevelt* (Cambridge, MA: Harvard University Press, 1972), 92–147; Raymond Moley, *The First New Deal* (New York: Harcourt, Brace & World, 1966), 14–17, 366–370.

22. Ellis W. Hawley, *The New Deal and the Problem of Monopoly: A Study in Economic Ambivalence* (Princeton, NJ: Princeton University Press, 1966), 149–186, 283–324; Donald Brand, *Corporatism and the Rule of Law: A Study of the National Recovery Administration* (Ithaca, NY: Cornell University Press, 1988), part I; Robert Himmelberg, *The Origins of the National Recovery Administration: Business, Government, and the Trade Association Issue* (New York: Fordham University Press, 1976), 43–74; Colin Gordon, *New Deals: Business, Labor, and Politics in America, 1920–1935* (New York: Cambridge University Press, 1994), 39–49, 128–159.

23. Michael E. Parrish, *Felix Frankfurter and His Times* (New York: The Free Press, 1982), 106–108, 199–204, 22–237; Frances Perkins, *The Roosevelt I Knew* (New York: Viking Press, 1946); Jordan A. Schwarz, *The New Dealers: Power Politics in the Age of Roosevelt* (New York: Alfred A. Knopf, 1993), 59–95; Jesse H. Jones, *Fifty Billion Dollars: My Thirteen Years with the RFC, 1932–1945* (New York: Macmillan, 1951).

24. Frank Freidel, *Franklin D. Roosevelt: A Rendezvous with Destiny* (Boston: Little, Brown, 1990), 63–78.

25. Roosevelt, ed., *F.D.R.: His Personal Letters*, 1928–1945, 329; Alter, *The Defining Moment*, 169–177; Frank Freidel, *Franklin D. Roosevelt: Launching the New Deal* (Boston: Little, Brown, 1973), 169–171.

26. *Time*, March 13, 1933; Alter, *The Defining Moment*, 214.

27. Susan Estrabook Kennedy, *The Banking Crisis of 1933* (Lexington: University of Kentucky Press, 1973), 77–178; William E. Leuchtenburg, *Franklin D. Roosevelt and the New Deal* (New York: Harper & Row, 1963), 39–40.

28. Rosenman, ed., *Public Papers and Addresses of Franklin D. Roosevelt*, 1933: 11–16.

29. Rosenman, ed., *Public Papers and Addresses of Franklin D. Roosevelt*, 1933: 61–65; Alter, *The Defining Moment*, 263–271.

30. Peter Temin, *Did Monetary Forces Cause the Great Depression?* (New York: W. W. Norton, 1976); Milton Friedman and Anna Jacobson Schwarz, *The Great Contraction, 1929–1933* (Princeton: Princeton University Press, 1965);

Hawley, *The New Deal and the Problem of Monopoly*, 395–397; Rosenman, ed., *Public Papers and Addresses of Franklin D. Roosevelt*, 1938: 41.

31. Raymond Moley, *After Seven Years: A Political Analysis of the New Deal* (New York: Harper, 1939), 155; Turner Catledge, "A Hard-Hitter Strikes at the Budget," *New York Times Magazine*, March 19, 1933, 3, 15; Alter, *The Defining Moment*, 275–276.

32. Freidel, *Launching the New Deal*, 470–489; Rosenman, ed., *Public Papers and Addresses of Franklin D. Roosevelt*, 1933: 264; *New York Times*, June 17, 18, 1933.

33. Richard Lowitt and Maurine Beaseley, eds., *One Third of a Nation: Lorena Hickok Reports on the Great Depression* (Urbana: University of Illinois Press, 1981); Donald Worster, *The Dust Bowl: The Southern Plains in the 1930s* (New York: Oxford University Press, 1979), 9–80; Timothy Egan, *The Worst Hard Time: The Untold Story of Those Who Survived the Great American Dust Bowl* (New York: Houghton Mifflin, 2006), 91–170; Grant McConnell, *The Decline of Agrarian Democracy* (New York: Atheneum, 1977), 10–65, 166–181; John L. Shover, *Cornbelt Rebellion: The Farmers' Holiday Association* (Urbana: University of Illinois Press, 1965), 132–167.

34. T. H. Watkins, *The Hungry Years: A Narrative History of the Great Depression in America* (New York: Henry Holt, 1999), 339–420; David M. Kennedy, *Freedom From Fear: The American People in Depression and War, 1929–1945* (New York: Oxford University Press, 1999), 190–212.

35. Hawley, *The New Deal and the Problem of Monopoly*, 19–52; Robert D. Cuff, *The War Industries Board: Business-Government Relations during World War I* (Baltimore: Johns Hopkins University Press, 1973); David M. Kennedy, *Over Here: The First World War and American Society* (New York: Oxford University Press, 1980), 126–143.

36. James MacGregor Burns, *Roosevelt: The Lion and the Fox, 1882–1940* (New York: Harcourt, Brace, Jovanovich, 1956), 181; Leuchtenburg, *Franklin D. Roosevelt and the New Deal*, 65–67.

37. Alan Brinkley, *Liberalism and Its Discontents* (Cambridge, MA: Harvard University Press, 1998), 27–30; Hawley, *The New Deal and the Problem of Monopoly*, 72–146; Kenneth Finegold and Theda Skocpol, "State Capacity and Economic Intervention in the Early New Deal," *Political Science Quarterly* 97, no. 2 (1982), 255–278; Kenneth Finegold and Theda Skocpol, *State and Party in America's New Deal* (Madison: University of Wisconsin Press, 1995).

38. *A. L. A. Schechter Poultry Corporation, et al. v. United States*, 295 U.S. 553 (1935); Moley, *After Seven Years*, 306–308.

39. Thomas K. McCraw, *TVA and the Power Fight, 1933–1939* (Philadelphia: J. B. Lippincott Company, 1971), 26–107.

40. Thomas K. McCraw, *Prophets of Regulation* (Cambridge, MA: Harvard University Press, 1984), 184–196.

41. Rosenman, ed., *Public Papers and Addresses of Franklin D. Roosevelt*, 1933: 420; Arthur M. Schlesinger Jr., *The*

Coming of the New Deal (Boston: Houghton Mifflin, 1959), 267; Anthony J. Badger, *The New Deal: The Depression Years, 1933–1940* (New York: Hill & Wang, 1989), 200–201.

42. Kennedy, *Freedom From Fear*, 144–147; John A. Salmond, *The Civilian Conservation Corps, 1933–1942* (Durham, NC: Duke University Press, 1967).

43. Kenneth T. Jackson, *The Crabgrass Frontier: The Suburbanization of the United States* (New York: Oxford University Press, 1985), 195–218; Leuchtenburg, *Franklin D. Roosevelt and the New Deal*, 53, 61.

44. Hofstadter, *The American Political Tradition*, 316; Moley, *After Seven Years*, 369–370; Alter, *The Defining Moment*, 302–308; Burns, *Roosevelt: The Lion and the Fox*, 287–288.

45. Robert F. Burk, *The Corporate State and the Broker State: The Du Ponts and American National Politics, 1925–1940* (Cambridge, MA: Harvard University Press, 1990), 143–191; Alan Brinkley, *Voices of Protest: Huey Long, Father Coughlin, and the Great Depression* (New York: Alfred A. Knopf, 1983).

46. Rexford G. Tugwell, *Roosevelt's Revolution: The First Year, a Personal Perspective* (New York: Macmillan, 1977), 59.

47. Leuchtenburg, *Franklin D. Roosevelt and the New Deal*, 124–130.

48. Theda Skocpol, *Protecting Soldiers and Mothers: The Political Origins of Social Policy in the United States* (Cambridge, MA: Harvard University Press, 1992); Linda Gordon, *Pitied But Not Entitled: Single Mothers and the History of Welfare* (New York: The Free Press, 1994), Kennedy, *Freedom From Fear*, 259–273.

49. Leon Keyserling, "The Wagner Act: Its Origin and Current Signficance," *George Washington Law Review* 29, no. 2 (1960), 200–208.

50. Roosevelt, ed., *F.D.R.: His Personal Letters*, 481–484; Mark Leff, *The Limits of Symbolic Reform: The New Deal and Taxation, 1933–1939* (New York: Cambridge University Press, 1984), 48–90.

51. Rosenman, ed., *Public Papers and Addresses of Franklin D. Roosevelt*, 1936: 566–573; Moley, *After Seven Years*, 352.

52. *The Nation*, November 7, 14, 1936; *The New Republic*, November 11, 1936; Sidney M. Milkis, "Franklin D. Roosevelt and the Transcendence of Party Politics," *Political Science Quarterly* 100, no. 3 (1985), 479–504.

53. William E. Leuchtenburg, *The Supreme Court Reborn: The Constitutional Revolution in the Age of Roosevelt* (New York: Oxford University Press, 1995), 82–162, 213–236; Alan Brinkley, Laura Kalman, William E. Leuchtenburg, and G. Edward White, "The Debate over the Constitutional Revolution of 1937," *American Historical Review* 110 (2005), 1046–1115.

54. Barry Karl, *Executive Reorganization and Reform in the New Deal* (Cambridge, MA: Harvard University Press, 1963), 166–265; Alan Brinkley, *The End of Reform: New Deal Liberalism in Recession and War* (New York: Alfred A. Knopf, 1995), 17–23.

55. Brinkley, *The End of Reform*, 23–20.

56. Alan Brinkley, "The Antimonopoly Ideal and the Liberal State: The Case of Thurman Arnold," *Journal of American History* 80, no. 2 (1993), 557–579; Corwin D. Edwards,

"Thurman Arnold and the Antitrust Laws," *Political Science Quarterly* 58, no. 3 (1943), 338–35; Richard Hofstadter, "What Happened to the Antitrust Movement? Notes on the Evolution of an American Creed," in Earl F. Cheit, ed., *The Business Establishment* (New York: John Wiley, 1964), 114; Hawley, *The New Deal and the Problem of Monopoly,* 402–420; Brinkley, *The End of Reform*, 122–131.

57. Alan Sweezy, "The Keynesians and Government Policy, 1933–1939," *American Economic Review* 62, no. 1–2 (1972), 117; Donald T. Critchlow, "The Political Control of the Economy: Deficit Spending as a Political Belief, 1932–1952," *The Public Historian* 3 (1981), 5–22.

58. James T. Patterson, *Congressional Conservatism and the New Deal: The Growth of the Conservative Coalition in Congress, 1933–1939* (Lexington: University of Kentucky Press, 1967), 211–324.

59. Robert Dallek, *Franklin D. Roosevelt and American Foreign Policy, 1932–1945* (New York: Oxford University Press, 1979), 52–58.

60. Dallek, *Franklin D. Roosevelt and American Foreign Policy*, 38–41, 84–85.

61. Rosenman, ed., *Public Papers and Addresses of Franklin D. Roosevelt*, 1933: 129–133.

62. Denna F. Fleming, *The United States and the World Court* (Garden City, NY: Doubleday, 1945); Brinkley, *Voices of Protest*, 134–137.

63. Warren F. Kimball, *The Juggler: Franklin Roosevelt as Wartime Statesman* (Princeton, NJ: Princeton University Press,

1991), 7–12; Dallek, *Franklin D. Roosevelt and American Foreign Policy*, 126–143, 158–162, 177–180.

64. Rosenman, ed., *Public Papers and Addresses of Franklin D. Roosevelt*, 1937: 406–411.

65. Dallek, *Franklin Roosevelt and American Foreign Policy*, 201–205; Kennedy, *Freedom from Fear*, 460–462.

66. Rosenman, ed., *Public Papers and Addresses of Franklin D. Roosevelt*, 1940: 193; Freidel, *Franklin D. Roosevelt*, 327–328, 342–345.

67. Wendell Willkie, "We the People," *Fortune*, April 1940; *Life*, May 13, 1940; Oren Root, *Persons and Persuasions* (New York: W. W. Norton, 1974), 20–36; Freidel, *Franklin D. Roosevelt*, 342–346.

68. Elting E. Morison, *Turmoil and Tradition: A Study of the Life and Times of Henry L. Stimson* (Boston: Houghton Mifflin, 1960), 477–482; Arthur M. Schlesinger, Jr. and Fred I. Israel, eds., *History of American Presidential Elections* (New York: Chelsea House, 1971), 4:2917–3006; Robert Sherwood, *Roosevelt and Hopkins: An Intimate History* (New York: Harper, 1948), 186–201; Rosenman, ed., *Public Papers and Addresses of Franklin D. Roosevelt*, 1940: 517.

69. Sherwood, *Roosevelt and Hopkins*, 221–229; Doris Kearns Goodwin, *No Ordinary Time: Franklin and Eleanor Roosevelt: The Home Front in World War II* (New York: Simon & Schuster, 1994), 190–196.

70. Kenneth S. Davis, *FDR: The War President, 1940–1943* (New York: Random House, 2000), 277–288.

71. Freidel, *Franklin D. Roosevelt*, 384–388; Joseph P. Lash, *Roosevelt and Churchill, 1939–1941: The Partnership that Saved the West* (New York: W. W. Norton, 1976), 398–400; Jon Meacham, *Franklin and Winston: An Intimate Portrait of an Epic Friendship* (New York: Random House, 2003); Raymond H. Dawson, *The Decision to Aid Russia, 1941* (Chapel Hill: University of North Carolina Press, 1959), 238–269.

72. John W. Dower, *War Without Mercy: Race and Power in the Pacific War* (New York: Pantheon, 1986), 100–112.

73. Rosenman, ed., *Public Papers and Addresses of Franklin D. Roosevelt*, 1941: 514–515.

74. Goodwin, *No Ordinary Time*, 485–504; Geoffrey C. Ward, ed., *Closest Companion: The Unknown Story of the Intimate Friendship between Franklin Roosevelt and Margaret Suckley* (New York: Houghton Mifflin, 1995), ix–xx, 191–420.

75. Goodwin, *No Ordinary Time*, 433–435, 499–500, 517–521.

76. Sherwood, *Roosevelt and Hopkins*, parts II and III.

77. "Documents Related to Churchill and FDR" (Washington, DC: U.S. National Archives and Records Administration); Francis L. Loewenheim, et al., eds., *Roosevelt and Churchill: Their Secret Wartime Correspondence* (New York: Saturday Review Press, 1975), 11–207.

78. *Time*, January 26, 1942; *Life*, January 26, 1942; Brinkley, *The End of Reform*, 174–191.

79. John Morton Blum, *V Was for Victory: Politics and American Culture During World War II* (New York: Harcourt, Brace, Jovanovich, 1976), 227–228.

80. Paul A. C. Koistinen, "Warfare and Power Relations in America: Mobilizing the World War II Economy," in James Titus, ed., *The Home Front and War in the Twentieth Century: The American Experience in Comparative Perspective* (Proceedings of the Tenth Military History Symposium, Colorado Springs, CO: United States Air Force Academy and Office of Air Force History, USAF, 1984), 104–105; "Dollar-a-Year Men," *Business Week*, April 12, 1941; Bruce Catton, *War Lords of Washington* (New York: Harcourt, Brace, 1948), 120–122, 177.

81. Rosenman, ed., *Public Papers and Addresses of Franklin D. Roosevelt*, 1944: 40–42; Kathleen Frydl, *The GI Bill* (New York: Cambridge University Press, 2009), 36–99; Brinkley, *The End of Reform*, 258–260.

82. Eleanor Roosevelt, "Race, Religion, and Prejudice," *The New Republic*, May 11, 1942, 630; Herbert Garfinkel, *When Negroes March: The March on Washington Movement in the Organizational Politics for FEPC* (Glencoe, IL: The Free Press, 1959); Horace R. Cayton, "The Negro's Challenge," *The Nation*, July 3, 1943, 10–12; Jervis Anderson, *Bayard Rustin: Troubles I've Seen* (New York: Harper Collins, 1997), 84–88.

83. U. S. Army, Western Defense Command, *Final Report, Japanese Evacuation from the West Coast, 1942* (Washington: Government Printing Office, 1943); *Korematsu v. United States*, 323 U.S. 214 (1944); Peter Irons, *Justice at War: The Story of the Japanese American Internment Cases* (New York: Oxford University Press, 1983), 6–75; Kai Bird, *The Chair-*

man: John J. McCloy and the Making of the American Establishment (New York: Simon & Schuster, 1992), 153–156.

84. Randolph Paul, "Report to the Secretary [of the Treasury] on the Acquiescence of This Government in the Murder of the Jews, January 13, 1944," in Richard D. Polenberg, *The Era of Franklin D. Roosevelt, 1933–1945: A Brief History with Documents* (Boston: Bedford/St.Martin's, 2000), 219–220; David S. Wyman, *The Abandonment of the Jews: America and the Holocaust, 1941–1945* (New York: Pantheon, 1984).

85. *Time*, July 24, 1944; Doris Kearns Goodwin, *No Ordinary Time*, 524–530.

86. Robert H. Ferrell, *The Dying President: Franklin D. Roosevelt, 1944–1945* (Columbia: University of Missouri Press, 1998); Goodwin, *No Ordinary Time*, 572–573; Rosenman, ed., *Public Papers and Addresses of Franklin D. Roosevelt, 1944–45*: 290.

87. Richard Rhodes, *The Making of the Atomic Bomb* (New York: Simon & Schuster, 1986).

88. James MacGregor Burns, *Roosevelt: The Soldier of Freedom, 1940–1945* (New York: Harcourt, Brace, Jovanovich, 1970), 558–592; Rosenman, ed., *Public Papers and Addresses of Franklin D. Roosevelt, 1944–45*: 511–514.

89. Rosenman, ed., *Public Papers and Addresses of Franklin D. Roosevelt, 1944–45*: 522–527; Freidel, *Franklin D. Roosevelt,* 602–607.

90. *New York Times*, April 13, 1945.

Bibliography

The Franklin D. Roosevelt Papers are housed in the Roosevelt Presidential Library in Hyde Park, N.Y., along with the papers of many other New Dealers. *The Public Papers and Addresses of Franklin D. Roosevelt*, ed. Samuel Rosenman, published in two multivolume series (1938, 1941), contains speeches and other official documents through 1940. Elliott Roosevelt, *F.D.R.: His Personal Letters, 1928–1945* (2 vols., 1950) offers a large selection of Roosevelt's correspondence.

Biographies of Roosevelt are numerous. Among them are Frank Freidel, *Franklin D. Roosevelt* (4 vols., 1952–1973) and *Franklin D. Roosevelt: A Rendezvous with Destiny* (1990); James MacGregor Burns, *Roosevelt: The Lion and the Fox* (1956) and *Roosevelt: The Soldier of Freedom* (1970); Joseph P. Lash, *Eleanor and Franklin* (1971); Geoffrey Ward, *Before the Trumpet* (1985) and *A First-Class Temperament* (1989); Kenneth S. Davis, *FDR* (5 vols., 1972–2000); Conrad Black, *Franklin*

Delano Roosevelt: Champion of Freedom (2003); Roy Jenkins, *Franklin Delano Roosevelt* (2003); Jean Edward Smith, *FDR* (2007); and H.W. Brands, *Traitor to His Class: The Privileged Life and Radical Presidency of Franklin Delano Roosevelt* (2008). An important biography of Eleanor Roosevelt is Blanche Wiesen Cook, *Eleanor Roosevelt: A Life* (2 vols., 1992–1999).

There are many memoirs and diaries of the Roosevelt years by those who served with him. Among the most important are Raymond Moley, *After Seven Years* (1939) and *The First New Deal* (1966); Rexford Tugwell, *The Democratic Roosevelt* (1957), *The Brains Trust* (1968), *In Search of Roosevelt* (1972), and *Roosevelt's Revolution* (1977); James A. Farley, *Behind the Ballots* (1938); Harold Ickes, *The Secret Diary of Harold Ickes* (3 vols., 1953–1954); Frances Perkins, *The Roosevelt I Knew* (1946); Grace Tully, *F.D.R.: My Boss* (1949); Edward J. Flynn, *You're the Boss* (1947); John Morton Blum, *From the Morgenthau Diaries* (3 vols., 1959–1967); Robert Sherwood, *Roosevelt and Hopkins* (1948); Henry L. Stimson and McGeorge Bundy, *On Active Service in Peace and War* (1948); and Eleanor Roosevelt, *This I Remember* (1949).

Among the many important studies of the New Deal are Arthur M. Schlesinger Jr., *The Age of Roosevelt* (3 vols., 1957–1960); William E. Leuchtenburg, *Franklin D. Roosevelt and the New Deal* (1963) and *The New Deal Years* (1995); David M. Kennedy, *Freedom From Fear: The American People in Depression and War* (1999); T. H. Watkins, *The Hungry Years* (1999); Anthony Badger, *The New Deal: The Depression Years, 1933–1940* (1989); Ellis Hawley, *The New Deal and the Problem of*

Monopoly (1966); Alan Brinkley, *The End of Reform: New Deal Liberalism in Recession and War* (1995); Steve Fraser and Gary Gerstle, eds., *The Rise and Fall of the New Deal Order* (1989); Colin Gordon, *New Deals* (1994); and Jonathan Alter, *The Defining Moment* (2006).

U.S. State Department, *Foreign Relations of the United States* (vols. 32–82, 1933–1945), Edgar B. Nixon, ed., *Franklin D. Roosevelt and Foreign Affairs* (3 vols., 1969), and David Schewe, ed., *Franklin D. Roosevelt and Foreign Affairs, January 1937–August 1939* (11 vols., 1979–1983) are important archival sources for the Roosevelt years. Major studies of Roosevelt's diplomacy include Robert Dallek, *Franklin D. Roosevelt and American Foreign Policy, 1932–1945* (1979), Warren Kimball, *The Juggler* (1991), and Jon Meacham, *Franklin and Winston* (2003). Doris Kearns Goodwin, *No Ordinary Time* (1994), is an intimate portrait of the Roosevelts during World War II.

For assessments of Roosevelt's posthumous legacy, see Robert Eden, ed., *The New Deal and Its Legacy* (1989), and William E. Leuchtenburg, *In the Shadow of FDR* (1983). Otis Graham and Meghan Robinson Wander, *Franklin D. Roosevelt: His Life and Times: An Encyclopedic View* (1985), is a valuable reference work.